JOHN SAINSBURY'S
GUIDE TO
WOODTURNING TOOLS
AND EQUIPMENT

JOHN SAINSBURY'S

GUIDE TO

WOODTURNING

TOOLS AND

EQUIPMENT

A DAVID & CHARLES CRAFT BOOK

Note: Sizes shown in the text are those quoted by the manufacturer. They are exact with approximate equivalents shown in brackets and nominated in imperial or metric.

British Library Cataloguing in Publication Data
Sainsbury, John A.
    John Sainsbury's guide to woodturning
    tools and equipment
    1. Wood turning. Manuals
    I. Title
    684'.08

    ISBN 0–7153–9336–7
    ISBN 0–7153–0212–4 Pbk

First published in paperback 1994

Typeset by ABM Typographics Ltd, Hull,
and printed in Great Britain
by Butler & Tanner Limited, Frome and London
for David & Charles Publishers plc
Brunel House   Newton Abbot   Devon

CONTENTS

INTRODUCTION

A history of woodturning has yet to be written, but it is certain that the craft is at least 5,000 years old. The earliest illustration was found in the tomb of an Egyptian priest called Petosirus. This has an approximate date of 300BC. It shows two men at work on a piece of timber that is mounted between two centres and revolved by a cord wrapped around it. A machine depicted on a stone cutter's gravestone of AD200 shows a similar device for turning a grinding wheel, though there is no evidence to prove that it was also a wood lathe. The treadle lathe did not appear for another thousand years and one example is of German origin. Here a pole is attached to a cord which is wrapped around the workpiece joined to a pedal. Turning, of course, could only take place when the pedal was pushed down and the workpiece turned towards the operator. The springiness of the pole returned the pedal to its upper position to allow further cutting.

Leonardo da Vinci drew a continuously rotating lathe using a treadle and flywheel. Here can be seen the first idea for a three point driving fork. That progress was slow is indicated by the fact that chair bodgers in England were still using the pole lathe at the beginning of this century. Ornamental lathes were designed and made by Holtzapfel and others in the nineteenth century but the greatest advances have been made in the last fifty years. Lathes were simple and the equipment made to hold and to drive material was basic. After World War II a great deal of pioneering work was done, particularly by Frank Pain, followed by Peter Child and his son, Roy. Nick Davidson became aware of the needs and developed a number of chucks.

Cutting tools, the chisel and the gouge, remained unchanged for centuries. Until recent years they were forged by the local blacksmith for the individual turner, or forged under spring hammers and ground by hand in the factories of Sheffield tool makers. The material used was carbon steel, the traditional material for woodcraft tools, and the shapes were largely those adopted by the tool maker with little reference to the user.

Great changes have taken place in recent times with the development of the craft and the considerable interest worldwide. Individual turners have explored the material and the design possibilities in so many ways, speeds of working have increased enormously and, as a result, both materials and methods of production have had to change to meet the challenge. We have seen the emergence of the listening manufacturers and to their credit they have produced high quality tools to a standard previously unknown. With such a proliferation of equipment there is a need for guidance and instruction. Manufacturers provide information with their equipment and there are many books on the subject, but often the authors tend to use and talk about the equipment with which they are familiar and few could spare the space to discuss fully the wide range of equipment now available. This book will give a better appreciation and satisfy a long felt need.

THE DREAM MACHINE

If we create the image of a dream machine it will serve to guide the would-be turner in his selection of the lathe best suited to his needs. Undoubtedly we shall have to accept that a dream which may bring pleasure to one turner may be another's nightmare. We must aim at a 'two feet on the ground' approach with the hope of dreaming up a machine that will meet the needs of the working craftsman at a realistic cost. Too often in the past lathes were designed by engineers with little contact with the user; indeed the user was often ignored. There is, however, a marked difference these days and lathes are being constructed and tested by men and women who know their business.

Lathes generally are a compromise; most users need to work both between centres and on the faceplate. This need will demand a range of speeds to take on varying sizes of work. Since most lathes have only four speeds, working through stepped pulleys, speeds for the large odd-shaped work are ignored, as also are those needed when turning tiny pieces. When looking at contemporary lathes only one has been designed specifically for bowl turning with the correct speeds; most other bowl turning lathes have been designed around the headstock of the full lathe, using the same speed arrangements.

Our dream machine must therefore solve the speed problem. A variable speed arrangement with foot control would be the ideal. Several methods of achieving this have been tried: some have been too expensive, others too heavy and cumbersome. Perhaps the best solution is the hydrostatic Speed Variator which will give an infinite variation of speed from 0 to the input speed. It has a high starting torque and high torque at low speeds with complete reversibility; acceleration and deceleration are under complete control. The Thompson lathe made in South Carolina has these features. Another method uses the spring-loaded variable-pitch motor pulley, which offers a continuous speed variation. Electronically variable speed is now available and is seen in the Delta lathe (see page 15). The moving cone system has been used in many metalworking applications and seems to be quite successful. Certainly, if we are to have the facility of speeds ranging from 250 to 4,000 rpm there must be a variable speed unit of some sort.

There is a call for a foot controlled clutch and a number of lathes have a hinged motor platform, which can be raised to allow the belt to run without driving; but there must be a better method, and our dream machine will need it if there is no foot controlled variable speed.

The weight of the lathe is very important, particularly when heavy work is being carried out and the bowl blank is running off-centre. It is inadvisable to bolt the machine to the floor for reasons detailed later; thus our lathe ought to have provision for sand or other weighty material to be poured into the casting, or for the addition of a sand box. It must, of course, have an arrangement for removing the sand.

Many lathes have large headstocks which make life difficult for the turner moving from left to right when turning between centres. Wherever possible sealed bearings should be used to house the running shaft. The latter should be bored right through and have a Morse taper. The spindle should be threaded at both ends even if there is no provision for an outboard attachment, since often it will be possible for a floor mounted toolrest pedestal to be installed. The drive system, including the motor, should be enclosed to reduce problems caused by dust and shavings. The drive in any case should be enclosed for safety. If motor and drive are housed in a pedestal then this must not prevent the left foot from taking up a comfortable stance, particularly when turning between centres. A stop/start reversing switch should be close to the left hand (since most people are right handed) with the provision of a foot switch, either pedal or dome, for emergency operation or, when, with the lathe running, it may be unsafe to remove one or other hand from the tool.

The lathe headstock should also have provision for a dividing head, which might also serve as a locking device for the spindle to assist in the removal of faceplates and chucks. Driving fork centres should have four chisels or points, preferably the latter, with the centre well forward of the leading edge of the chisels. The tailstock should be well built, with lever operation, which would save time, particularly when boring with tools held in the tailstock chuck. A useful addition would be a measured sleeve. There should be easy and positive locking, ensuring no slipping of the assembly along the lathebed. A running centre should be fitted as standard; the solid centre is outdated and lubrication for this often leaves a nasty smear on the work if too much is used. Toolrests have long been a problem; the turner of the past, using the lathe continuously, had a wooden rest, since it was warm to the touch and he could always reface it or make a new one in case of excessive wear. I have used this type for many years without problems (see page 94). The rest must be long and straight of curved section to fit the hand and the tool, with several lengths to suit individual needs. The rest should be bored for the insertion of pivot pins and fitted into a strong boss on the slide and must not prevent the rest from being brought up close across a bowl or plate. Clamping should be positive without obstructing the easy passage of the hand and tool across the rest. Clamping of the toolrest assembly itself should be easy and not require the use of spanners; that on the Graduate lathe is highly successful. Again, the type of lathe bed, which we hope would be solid grey iron with machined faces, will dictate the method of clamping. Other components should be in iron or steel. Beds of tube, rods and bars, often have problems in the alignment of centres.

Yes, it's a pretty formidable task. But with modern production methods and determination it should not be impossible to produce the dream machine, without making paupers of us all.

THE WOODTURNER'S WORKSHOP

All woodworking shops need good planning and none more so than that of the turner, whether he is working on his own in a home workshop or with others, on commercial lines: the requirements are the same.

A comfortable room in a heated building is perhaps the ideal, but often this is not possible because of noise and dust and then an outbuilding or wooden shed must be used. Wooden workshops are fine and I have used one for many years. This I insulated against heat losses, but the addition of double glazing was out of the question at the time. This would have given further protection and helped to reduce noise which might have annoyed the neighbours.

Good lighting is essential; large windows take up valuable wall space but are worthwhile. Artificial lighting must be good, and for general workshop purposes an adequate number of fluorescent tubes of the non-stroboscopic variety should be fitted. The lathe should have a flexible arm attached to or close by it, and a good tungsten bulb will help to throw light and shadow as necessary during the turning process. In the UK some manufacturers supply transformers with flexible arms to offer safe low-voltage lighting. In the USA most equipment will be 110 volt and safer than the 240v, which is common in the UK.

Flooring is important, and probably the best is the suspended type which must have adequate strength in the joists to support the weight of the machinery installed. If this is not possible and there are solid concrete floors, then these should be painted with a non-dusting, non-slip material. Concrete tends to be tough on the legs and feet after long standing and the use of flooring grade particle board on which to place the lathe and give adequate standing area is suggested. It will tend to polish over a period of time and may need to be given a non-slip coating. One of the best ideas I have seen is in the use of pieces of discarded conveyer belt from a local coal mine – extremely heavy but superb standing for both lathe and operator. A good floor will deaden noise and make for comfortable working.

Heating must be given a degree of priority; cold conditions are dangerous as cold hands lose their sensitivity, production is slowed, and enjoyment of the craft is lessened.

Centrally heated premises are the answer but this may not be possible or indeed economic. Open gas heaters produce a great deal of moisture, rusting the tools. Perhaps the best solution is an electric storage heater. These are much cheaper and smaller than they were many years ago. The key must be to look after the worker and also the tools. Electrical connections must be to a very high standard, be installed by an expert, and comply with safety precautions. Ideally a three phase system is needed where there are many machines in a production workshop, but the cost is prohibitive for the home workshop or even the small production shop with one or two turners. All machines should have a wall isolator switch, and cable should be carried in conduit or flexible metal sheathing. If there are 13 amp plugs, they should be correctly fused. The lathe should have approved fully-protected switching so that both machine and worker are safe from electric shock.

The lathe must be positioned to give adequate access at both ends and in front. If there is an outboard, then the lathe must be well away from a wall to allow the turner to move freely into any cutting position. The tailstock must be clear of any obstruction to allow the insertion of the long hole boring auger. Some people work both in front of and behind the lathe, and adequate space must be allowed to make

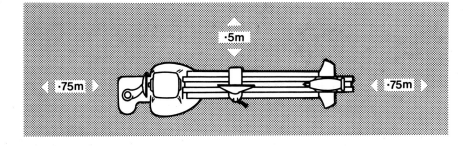

1 Positioning the lathe

this possible. The diagram shows the minimum spaces (Fig 1). The lathe should not be fixed to the floor, but weighted. The purpose-designed bowl turning lathe from Woodfast in Australia has a weight box which can be filled with heavy sand or similar material. Very heavy lathes will be stable enough even under load, but the bolting down of the lathe will only result in bearing damage if the workpiece is unevenly balanced.

The lathe centres must also be set to suit the turner. They should be at the same height from the floor as the point of the turner's elbow. This lessens the problem of aching backs. If the lathe is of the pedestal type, it may need to be raised on two stout blocks of timber. Care should be taken in sizing these so that they will not change the stance of the operator or render the lathe unsuitable.

Should the lathe be of the benchtop variety, a bench must be designed not only to meet the needs of the lathe, but also to be of manageable proportions and size to suit the individual. It can be constructed in timber – the legs should be stout and the top at least 2in (50mm) thick. If the bench is designed with drawers and cupboards, these must allow adequate knee/leg room for the turner. This storage space should house equipment and tools soundly so as to avoid noisy rattles.

My Avon lathe is fitted to a bench made in steel square and angle material with a 2in (50mm) thick top. The rear half of the top is of thinner material providing a space for tools in use. This is heavy enough for stability without being too heavy for me to move.

The mini-turning specialist who works in the spare room may care to make a bench fitted with a removable cover for the lathe itself. This would not be obtrusive and if made in a good hardwood might be acceptable even to the most fussy housewife. The

workshop should be provided with at least one cupboard to house all the accessories; it should be purpose designed with a position for each piece. Such a cupboard will keep the chucks and other machine pieces free from dust and chips particularly if they are cleaned before replacing. Spanners, knocking out bars and other tools used constantly must be housed on a board close to the lathe, but not on the wall immediately behind it – if they should fall they will fall to the floor clear of moving parts. Cutting tools are best kept in an open rack fixed to the wall or on a movable stand that can be placed close at hand when turning (see illustration p 149). Space must also be found for abrasive papers, cleaning and polishing cloths, fillers, polishes and steel wool. The accessories cupboard should also house the electric drill and flexible shaft if these are used by the turner. The aim should be to have as little as possible on open shelves and nothing above the lathe. A useful addition is a small blackboard which can be seen from the lathe, screwed to the wall and used for sketches and reminders.

Communications are always difficult; wives become angry when the lunch is spoiling – or when someone needs you on the phone and it is raining cats and dogs. I have installed an FM intercom which plugs into the mains system giving two-way communication – my wife can even talk to me without lifting the receiver (which may be a disadvantage). With phones everywhere nowadays, the installation of the standard telephone might be an advantage – for taking orders and facilitating quick communication with others. Luxuries, perhaps, but they do save a lot of hassle.

Dust extraction in these days of strange timbers and even stranger allergies is vital and it is as well to consider the installation of one of the many systems available.

Woodfast in Australia have a specially designed dust-extraction unit, which can be fitted to most lathes. I use a wall unit which can be linked to any of the machines. Total extraction of dust and chips from the lathe is practically impossible due to the movement of air around the machine, and so individual protection is necessary. This is discussed in chapter 11.

Timber should be stored away from the workshop – except the material for immediate use. Logs and planks should be sealed and only converted and brought into the working area when needed.

A small bench should be provided to house the machines and stones used for grinding and sharpening. They should be covered to protect them from shavings and dust. Again, I have constructed a bench using angle iron with a wooden top; on this I house the belt grinder and a rubberised wheel running horizontally, which I use for sharpening.

A small cupboard, clearly marked with a red cross on a white background, should be placed within easy access of the turner to house a complement of first aid equipment.

Shields, protective spectacles, ear muffs, facemasks and filters should be kept in a cupboard away from the dust and available for immediate use. Filters should be kept in dust free containers. Where work is removed from the lathe for polishing, a clean area should be set aside in the shop if one is not available elsewhere.

WOODTURNING

Note: Sizes shown in the text are those quoted by the manufacturer. They are exact with approximate equivalents shown in brackets and nominated in imperial or metric.

The essential kit
Tools, preferably of high speed, should include one of each of the following:

1in (25mm) skew chisel for planing

½in (12mm) skew chisel for shaping curves and making decorative cuts

¼in (6mm) chisel ground square across (beading chisel)

⅛in (3mm) parting tool

⅜in (10mm) long and strong gouge (bowl turning gouge) deep section, rounded nose

⅜ or ¼in (10 or 6mm) new style gouge for spindle work

¾in (19mm) roughing gouge (ground square across for roughing work between centres)

to which could be added

¼in (6mm) spindle gouge

The lathe
3 and 4in (75 and 100mm) faceplates

a combination chuck

to which can be added

1 screw chuck and faceplate rings of size to suit the expanding jaws of the chuck

A screw chuck is an essential piece of equipment and if a multi-purpose chuck is not available a screw chuck should be.

Additional equipment
lace bobbin drive for driving small pieces between centres

running centre

long hole boring tool ⅜in (10mm) with a long hole boring attachment to suit the lathe

1 each saw tooth cutters 2in (50mm) and 1 ¾in (44mm)

1 each flatbits 1½, 1¼, 1, ¾, and ½in (37, 31, 25, 19 and 12mm)

3

CHOOSING YOUR LATHE

Lathes rarely wear out; indeed bearings seem to be the only problem. Thus care should be taken in selecting a lathe which in all probability will be available for your grandchildren to use. Lathes fall into two groups:

☐ pedestal lathes (floor standing)

☐ bench types, which require a stand, bought or made.

They can have, in the case of the bench types:
☐ fixed headstocks

☐ a rotating head which can be set at any angle to the line of centres and at both 90° and 180° it becomes an outboard.
☐ a sliding head which is normally in the left hand position. However, it can be moved along to the right hand end of the bed for faceplate work, after removing the tailstock.

The fixed headstock can have a double-ended spindle so that an outboard turning attachment can be added with the obvious disadvantage that it requires both right and left hand accessories, thus adding to the cost.

Usually the pedestal type lathe will have a totally enclosed motor and drive. This is a great advantage in keeping the motor and drive free from shavings and dust and also in avoiding the necessity for belt guards.

Bench lathes will generally have guards fitted and lathes like the Myford where the motor is slung underneath it will be protected within the stand.

Drives can have a single vee or multi-vee pulleys, the latter providing a very positive drive. Access to the belt change mechanism varies, as does the method of locking. Generally manufacturers recognise the need for access and safety guards. Various types of locking levers are found, and they need to be of size and shape to make them easy on the hands.

Beds can be of single tube, twin tube, single and double solid rod, slotted tube, solid drawn square section bar, solid cast iron or aluminium alloy, or they can be prefabricated from steel or alloy. The solid cast beds can be machined accurately, will give extended use and are to be preferred. There are however prefabricated machines that are extremely good. Some alloy beds are far too light and weight is very important. Some beds – particularly those in the round – present problems in lining up the centres and slotted tubes get filled with shavings.

The tailstock and cross slide are best secured using a lever operated cam as in the Graduate lathe, but this is not possible on some other machines. Positive placement is essential. The advancement of the tailstock centre is effected by the use of a hand wheel or a lever; the latter is probably better. The hand wheel should be large enough to make for easy turning. Take a good look around the exhibitions, then find a stockist who knows his lathe business. Get all the answers, consider the cost and what you are getting for the money, then decide. Alternatively, take one of the courses available and do all your buying afterwards. You will then have a clearer picture of turning requirements and know if you will enjoy turning. If you are considering the purchase of a secondhand machine check the following points:

How old is the machine? Who used it? Was it used daily over a long period? Was it used for heavy or light work? Under what conditions was it stored?

Look first at the area around the bearings. If there is evidence of oil leaks, then the bearings could be worn or the sealed units cracked.

Hold the spindle firmly and see if you can move it by wrenching forward and back. If there is slack, then working problems can arise – it could need a new shaft or bearings.

Examine the bed for wear, chips or cracks and for evidence of abuse. Slide the tailstock backwards and forwards to see if it moves easily without slackness. This also applies to the toolrest slide. Check also that they lock satisfactorily. Check the sleeve of the tailstock for lateral movement.

Check the driving fork and dead centres for wear and move the tailstock – with the centre inserted – up to the headstock, and check its alignment with a pointed centre set in the spindle. If there is a problem check that re-alignment is possible.

Examine the spindle threads for wear.

Check all levers for perfect action.

Look carefully at the motor to see that the connections are not frayed, that it has been kept clean with the grease caps full. Look also to see that adjustment is possible on the slides or in any other method of mounting which may be used. Check the condition of the belt and, if worn, see that the fitting of a new one will not create any problems for you. Try the motor under load. Check the switch.

Examine all the extras such as faceplates, chucks etc, to see that they fit the machine.

Be very careful to make sure that the threading on the spindle is standard; it would be annoying to buy a machine and find that none of the chucks and other devices then on offer can be matched to it. (The leading makers of chucks usually stock unthreaded bodies to meet this situation, but having them threaded will add to the cost.) A close examination of the cutting tools will give some indication of the former owner's care since, in the hands of a good craftsman, they will be well looked after and carefully housed.

Paintwork on the lathe is often a good indication of the amount of use it has had and the care which has been taken with it. A newly painted old machine might well need more careful examination than one with old paintwork.

Some manufacturers number their machines, and it may be possible to check this. The number of my Harrison Graduate lathe is found at the right hand end of the bed, and I am quite sure that not only would Harrisons be able to tell me when it was made but also to whom it was despatched.

Having considered the dream machine and the different styles of lathe, now take a close look at the many lathes on offer. There is a wide choice. Check that any lathe under consideration is made by a brand leader with good stocks of spares (not that lathes generally need many spares), but also that there is good after sales service. There are many cases of 'sell and forget' and the buyer could be in trouble. An examination of the craft press will soon indicate the reliable manufacturer and knowledgeable stockists. It is also a good plan to look up the reports, written by leading turners and printed in the woodworking magazines. Visit some of the leading turners, talk to one or two if at all possible and see which machines they are using.

Perhaps the most exciting lathe to be launched in recent times is the Delta DL40 electronic variable speed machine which must be well ahead of all others. The basic unit comprises a cast iron bed with a totally enclosed headstock. The bed accepts 52 in (1,320mm) between centres with a 16in (406mm) swing over. Large diameter work can be carried out using the outboard spindle and standard equipment outboard table ledge. Both spindles have No 2 Morse taper with 1in (25mm) 8RH thread inboard and 1in (25mm) 8LH thread outboard. The spindle locks to facilitate faceplate mounting and there is a 36-point indexing mechanism. Standard equipment includes a two panel safety shield which adjusts to cover work at either spindle; drive and cup centres; 6in (150mm), 12in (300mm) toolrests and a unique French curl rest for bowl work. The toolrest support has a three position locking lever and there are 3in (75mm) and 6in (150mm) faceplates. A heavy cabinet stand is also available with numerous other accessories.

Electronics suggest untold complexities, but the reader should not be dismayed since in use the system is quite simple. It consists of a two-in-one processor; the master is tied directly into a control box and a slave processor interprets the commands given to it for the motor drive. Speeds range from 300 to 2,200rpm with 300 to 1,000rpm in reverse. When under load the processor will instruct the motor to compensate with additional power thus maintaining a constant torque on the working piece. It offers both normal and slow start modes. In each case the speed can be increased or decreased while the spindle is turning. A single touch alters speeds in

2 Delta DL electronic variable speed lathe

3 Lathe viewed from the tailstock

4 Lathe control box

5 Delta French curve bowl rest

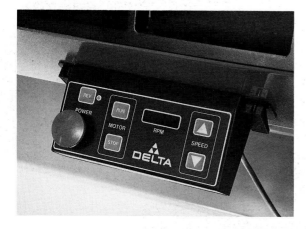

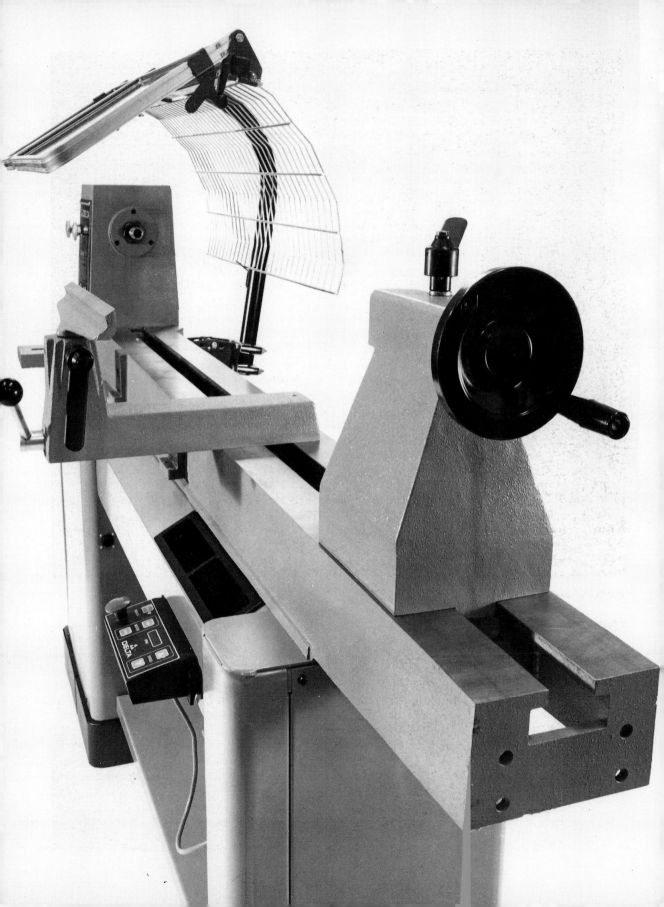

increments of 10rpm, while steady pressure changes speed in 100rpm units. When operating in the normal mode, speed can also be preset before starting spindle rotation. In addition, the spindle will resume the speed at which it was stopped. For teaching workshops the slow start mode limits spindle speed to 300rpm each time it is set to run, allowing speed increases only when the spindle is turning. The machine can be set in either the normal or slow-start mode by operating a toggle switch at the rear of the machine and a padlock can be used to lock it if desired. The motor speed is evaluated 120 times per second, and this ensures perfect torque to match the turning being done. The speed is seen on the LED readout. The microprocessor is turned on by pulling the red button which also serves as the emergency stop. When the machine starts it runs at 300rpm, thus reducing considerably the brush wear and the mechanical stresses on motor and machine. Speed arrows on the operating panel adjust the speed either way and once the speed is shown on the readout the turner presses the run button. If a stop is needed for examination of the work, the machine will return to its nominated running speed. The whole business takes seconds and never again will mechanical adjustments have to be made. The electronics will detect if the lathe is locked by the indexing pin and wait for a second until it is released and then either stop or reset. The system is not affected by current surges; other fail safe devices are incorporated. A 1hp DC motor is supplied for the States assuring constant torque on the workpiece. Here may well be the birth of our dream machine.

We have long waited for a manufacturer to produce a bowl turning lathe that has the features such work demands. So-called bowl lathes have always been a compromise. The maker took an existing full facilities lathe and adapted it, ignoring the fact that a bowl lathe needs different speeds from those for spindle work, and that the weight required to keep the lathe steady and reduce vibration is quite considerable. Fortunately Woodfast Machinery in Woodville, South Australia, in conjunction with Howard Lewin, an active turner in the United States have produced what looks like the answer. The BL 300 has been designed as a specialised bowl turning lathe, with a range of low speeds to suit the tasks it is likely to be given. The lathe bed, head, and tailstock, are precision machined cast iron. The all-steel cabinet is sturdily constructed, incorporating a bottom drawer – not for storing a daughter's premarital gifts, but to fill with sand or other heavy material to add weight at the base of the machine. Very sturdy toolrests and brackets are adequate for the task and turning facilities are available at both ends. With the present trend toward turning bowls from roughcut timber, leaving the natural edge, the original turning blank is often out of round and greatly varied in density. This can cause massive vibration and unless a machine is designed for this then turning can be dangerous. It is also possible on this lathe to fit a tailstock and 12in (305mm) can be turned between centres. The tailstock can be used to support heavy work at the outset of turning, as well as for boring. The headstock incorporates a sturdy drive shaft with five large 72mm (3in) diameter sealed bearings giving vibration-free turning even with the heaviest of cuts.

Both the tailstock and the toolrest bracket have a camlock device for instant and positive locking.

A straight toolrest is standard and a heavy duty curved rest is available for bowl work. The lathe swing-over size is 16½in (420mm), and rear turning capacity is 24in (610mm). The tailstock spindle is bored No 2 Morse taper and has 4in (100mm) of travel. Height from floor to centre of spindle is 45in (1,150mm). Spindle speeds are just right 250, 470, 800 and 1,300rpm. Spindle threads are 30mm×3.5P for metricated areas while 1in×8tpi is available for the USA and Canada. The motor is 1hp, single phase with a magnetic contactor safety switch. The motor and quick speed change tensioning gear are housed in a compartment with a safety door. Alongside is a compartment holding the operating switch, suitably positioned for easy access. This compartment is available for turning equipment.

This is a genuine attempt to solve many of the problems of the bowl turner; with one or two of our dream-machine features it could be even better.

Woodfast also have two excellent lathes the MC900 and the MC900s suitable for professionals and serious amateurs.

A bowl turning lathe, which is again a complete departure from those previously designed, comes from another company manufacturing in Australasia. Tanner Engineering, with the GB 165 (Fig 7), has

6 Woodfast BL bowl lathe

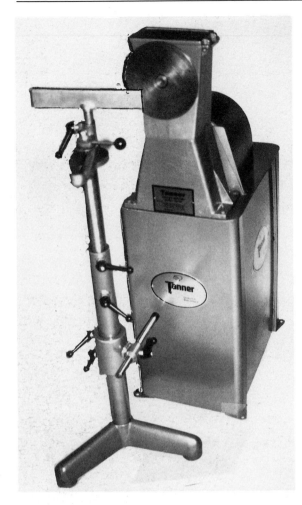

7 Tanner GB 165 bowl lathe

The choice of speeds available to the turner is a tremendous advantage. The transmission is through a five-speed alpha section vee belt to double 'A' section notched vee belt final drive and the buyer may specify one of four options when purchasing his lathe. I believe this to be a world 'first'. The options are as follows:

A	80	130	190	330	500
B	100	160	225	410	620
C	120	200	225	410	750
D	160	260	380	660	1000

Such a choice of speeds simply means that, from the man turning large table tops to the average turner of bowls, there is an exact choice – something unheard of previously for faceplate work. This is all matched with the design of a heavy adjustable tripod toolrest assembly which slides toward or away from the lathe on a steel bar. This is designed to allow for full adjustment to take in every option of work size. The lathe is fitted with a push button starter with no volt release and overload. Another 'first' is a pull cord on/off switch for overhead operation (I would have preferred a floor switch for foot operation, since both hands may be occupied when an emergency arises). A full range of accessories is available.

Space will not permit every lathe to be described in detail but the table which follows gives most of the basic information to enable the craftsman to select some which may meet his needs – he can then obtain full details from the manufacturer or merchant and have a demonstration before making a final choice.

LATHES FOR MINIATURE WORK

Very few lathes have been designed specifically for the miniaturist; indeed, many turners might question the need since tiny work can be turned on a lathe of any size. Many people choose however to work 'in the small' and would never need to use a large lathe; many choose this area of activity because of lack of space.

Some lathes quoted as ideal for the miniaturist are merely sized-down versions of existing lathes. Manufacturers, until recent years, have tended to ignore the need for miniaturist equipment such as drives and chucks – thus often obliging the user to design

produced a completely new design. The company has used its experience in producing standard lathes but has stoutly resisted being compromised in any way by using existing components and has brought about a purpose-designed job with a number of innovative features.

The lathe is very heavy, ideal for bowls, with a massive solid steel spindle running in heavy-duty sealed bearings. The spindle is threaded at the right hand end 1½in (38mm)×6tpi and left plain, 40mm diameter at the left hand end. The headstock is of cast iron with a hinged cover and hinged pulley guard. The motor is mounted on a lever operated clamp and totally enclosed.

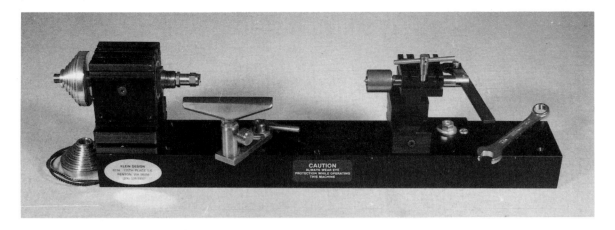

8 Klein lathe

9 Klein bowl turning head

his own. One such turner is Miss Bonnie Klein of Washington and the Klein lathe made by Anker Engineering in Oregon is arguably the best. An active turner with a special flair for tiny work, Miss Klein has studied the problems and provided most of the answers (Figs 8, 9). Hers is a quality lathe, precision built for long life and reliability. The headstock has its spindle running in ball bearings guaranteed for life, with a six-step pulley and vee belt. A ¼hp motor with standard revolutions will give speeds of approximately 600, 1,000, 1,400, 2,300, and 5,200rpm which will cover every eventuality. The hollow spindle is threaded ¾ × 16tpi. The lathe will accept stock 5in (125mm) diameter and up to 12in (305mm) long. The tailstock is an end-drilling type threaded to receive a Jacobs chuck or a deluxe running centre with two inserts. The hollow spindle permits long stock to be inserted and held in collets of which there are eight different sizes. The tailstock has an Allen screw for adjustment located on the right hand side for alignment of centres and also for use when offset turning is undertaken.

The toolrest is of hardened steel, fully adjustable with two levers for locking.

The lathe bed is accurately made and a wrench is supplied for fixing the tailstock. It is suggested that the lathe be fitted with a ¼hp motor and pulleys are supplied for either ¼ or ⅜in (6mm and 10mm) shafts.

An arbor is supplied to which the spur drive and other accessories can be screwed and held through the hollow headstock spindle.

The lathe comes ready for assembly with full instructions and it is suggested that the bed be fastened

down with four bolts to a stout board. It is an excellent idea to build it into a carrying case and make provision for the motor to be fitted within the case; this will also help in getting the lathe to the best working height.

Every conceivable accessory is available including a faceplate, supplied as standard, which screws onto the spindle and has four holes for fixing. Accessories are three and four jaw chucks, a set of eight collets, drill chuck arbor threaded ⅜×24tpi for a Jacobs drill chuck, a set of eight collets, ⅜ and ¼in (10 and 6mm) drill chucks, cone chuck, screw centre, three deep hole drilling guides and a Yankee chucker for square wood stock 1/16 to ¼in (1.5 to 6mm). A spigot/collet chuck can also be fitted.

MAKER AND COUNTRY OF ORIGIN	MODEL IDENTIFICATION	HEIGHT OF CENTRES	BETWEEN CENTRES	POWER HP	SPEED rpm	TYPE OF DRIVE	TYPE OF BED	GAP BED	WEIGHT kg	MORSE TAPER NO	OUTBOARD TURNING FACILITY	ADDITIONAL FEATURES
ALKO WEST GERMANY	HDM 850	120	900	3/4	3 / 950-2,100	V	2 □ Bars	155	36	—	—	
APOLLO UK	Woodpecker	140	815	1/2	4 / 460-2,000	Poly V	2 □ Bars	760 x 230	55	1	—	Swivelling headstock – 405mm Duplicator available
ARNALL AUSTRALIA	N/A	250	Optional	1	5	V	Rolled Steel	760 x 235 Section infill	—	2	—	Collet chuck. Gate toolrest and special purpose designed calipers and tools for limited aperture turning
ARUNDEL UK	KA450	115	840	1/2	4 / 500-2,150	Poly V	2 ● Bars	—	42	1	—	Headstock slides to right hand end of bed for outboard turning with capacities of 460, 560, 560 maximum
	K450 HD	115	915	1/2	7 / 500-1,250	Poly V	2 ● Bars	—	49	1	—	
	K600	115	915	3/4	375-2,200	Poly V	2 ● Bars	—	50	1	—	
CORONET UK	No 1 / No 3	150	610	1/2	3 / 450-2,000	Poly V	2 ● Bars	Yes	67	1	—	Kit available to convert to gap bed
	Elf	76	762	1/2	4 / 425-2,000	Poly V	1 ● Bar	—	42	1	—	Patented. Swivelling headstock
	Major	115	838	3/4	5 / 425-2,000	Poly V	1 ● Bar	—	64	1	—	Chucks. Swivelling headstock
CONOVER USA		200	Unlimited	1-1½	4 / 600-2,600	V	Timber bed	—	180	No 3 in headstock No 2 in tailstock	—	Timber bed not supplied. Headstock indexed
CENTAURO ITALY	1200 TM 1600 2000	250	1,200/2,000	3	600-3,000		CI Frame	—	390	2	—	Floor standing. Copying attachment
DELTA USA	DL 40	406 Overtool rest 304	1,320	1¼	Forward 300-2,200 reverse 300-1,000	Electronic variable speed no belt	CI Machined	—	220	2 / —	Yes	Superchuck. Microprocessor control with slow and normal soft start
DENFORD UK	TD56WL (Senior)	150	914	3/4 or 1¼	4 / 425-2,275	Linked belt	CI Machined	—	228	3	Yes	Pedestal lathe, short bed and bowl turning head options
DOMINION UK	FJA	150	762	1	Multispeed 400-2,200	Special	CI Machined	—	330	3	Yes up to 508	Pedestal lathe, varispeed using 2 cones spindle – foot brake
ELECTRA BECKUM WEST GERMANY	HDM 800	190	800	1/2	4 / 800-2,500	V belt with grooved pulley	2 ○ Bars	—	35	—	—	
WEST GERMANY	HDM 1000	190	1,000	3/4	4 / 800-2,500		2 ○ Bars	—	40	No 3 in tailstock	—	
ELU WEST GERMANY	DB 180	190	1,000	1½	3 / 800-2,350	V	2 ○ Bars	—	32	—	—	Toolrest has rolling bar
EMCO AUSTRIA	DB 6	200	1,000	1⅓	4 / 500-2,500	V	Steel fabricated	—	50	—	—	Revolving centre as standard

MAKER AND COUNTRY OF ORIGIN	MODEL IDENTIFICATION	HEIGHT OF CENTRES	BETWEEN CENTRES	POWER HP	SPEED rpm	TYPE OF DRIVE	TYPE OF BED	GAP BED	WEIGHT kg	MORSE TAPER NO	OUTBOARD TURNING FACILITY	ADDITIONAL FEATURES
HARRISON UK	Graduate	150	Options 760-1,370	3/4	4 425-2,250	V	CI Machined	—	228-280	No 3 in headstock No 2 in tailstock	up to 460	Short bed and bowl turning options bowl turning weight – 140 kg.
HOBBYMAT EAST GERMANY	Variant	120	650	1/2	3 950-2,100	V	2■Bars	—	30	No 1 in tailstock	—	Special chuck — Special chuck, revolving centre included lathe bed extension
HEGNER WEST GERMANY	HDB 175	175	770	3/4	4 800-2,800	V	Solid bar	—	50	No 2 in tailstock	—	Duplicator available for spindle and bowl work
	HDB 200	200	1,000	3/4	4 800-2,800	V		—	100	—	—	
KITY FRANCE	663	195	1,000 / 1,500	1	3 750-3,000	V	Aluminium channel All models	—	75 / 75	2	—	All models have revolving centres
	664	195	1,000 / 1,500	1	Variable speed	Cone drive		—	75 / 75	2	—	
LATALEX NEW ZEALAND	TL 1000/8S	310	970 or 1,220	1/2, 3/4, 1 optional	8 178-3,000	V	1□Tube	—	—	2	Yes 500 mm	Multichuck II Nova scroll — Indexing device. Outboard optional also stand
LUNA SWEDEN	SP 800	150	800	3/4	3 750-3,000	V	Steel fabricated	—	36	No 2 in tailstock	—	Spannofix and autofix chucks
	SP 1000	210	1,000	3/4	3 750-3,000	V	Steel fabricated	—	50	—	—	
	Avant 320	210	320	3/4	4 400-3,000	Poly V	Steel fabricated	—	38	—	—	
LUNA-MINIMAX ITALY	T 100	220	1,000	1	4 500-2,500	V	Steel fabricated	—	90	2	—	Weights quoted include the stand. Revolving centre included
	T 120	220	1,200	1		V	Steel fabricated	—	115	2	—	
LUNGRENS SWEDEN	N/A	400	700	3/4	380	V	2□Tube	—	90	No 2 in tailstock	—	Floor stand available
MERLIN UK	CM 25	200	600-1,200	1/2	4 650-3,000	V	1●Bar	—	—	1	Yes	Outboard turning available 450mm maximum
MULTISTAR UK	Maxima	230	460-965	1	5 200-2,850	V	Steel fabricated	—	150	2	—	Multistar chuck — Swivelling headstock Lathe can be personalised
MYFORD UK	ML 8	100	915 / 1,065	3/4	4 700-2,850	Linked belt	Slotted tube	—	35	1	Yes up to 305	4 in 1 chuck — Outboard available as an extra, also cabinet stand. Headstock pulley indexed
NAEROK	WL 600	255	600	1/2	4 850-2,620	Round belt	Steel fabricated	—	30	—	—	Revolving centre fitted
TAIWAN	WL 800	180	800	1/2	4 810-2,485	V	Steel fabricated	—	30	—	—	
	WL 1203T	150	940	3/4	5 483-3,012	V	1○Bar	—	—	1	Yes	
SYMTEC	1800	400	1,300	1 1/2	4 550-3,700	V	Machined	—	200	2	—	Indexing 24 holes
	1500	330	970	1	3 550-3,700	V	Wide flatbed	—	120	2	—	Cutting using a stylus also copying device

All sizes are quoted in metric.

■ – Solid square   ● – Solid round   □ – Tube   CI – Cast iron

MAKER AND COUNTRY OF ORIGIN	MODEL IDENTIFICATION	HEIGHT OF CENTRES	BETWEEN CENTRES	POWER HP	SPEED rpm	TYPE OF DRIVE	TYPE OF BED	GAP BED	WEIGHT kg	MORSE TAPER NO	OUTBOARD TURNING FACILITY	ADDITIONAL FEATURES
SCHEPPACH WEST GERMANY	DMV 200	205	880	1	5 410-2,800	V	Steel fabricated	—	90	—	—	Fitted with spindle brake. Bed extension available
SUMACO	TWL 800	200	800	3/4	5 550-2,500	V	2● Bars	—	79	Tailstock No 3	—	Weight includes stand in both. Fitted brake and revolving centre
TAIWAN	TWL 1000	200	1,000	1	5 550-2,500	V	2○ Bars	—	85	—	—	
TANNER	Tamecraft 300	153	950		4 450-3,900	V	1○ Bar	—	55	2	—	Motor not supplied
NEW ZEALAND	FS 100	165	1,030	1	5 460-3,100	V	CI Machined	450	76	2	—	Weight of bench machine. Complete machine 152 kg.
	GB 165	1,100 floor to spindle			5	V	Bowl lathe only	—	—	—	—	Four separate range options are available to choice, adjustable tripod toolrest, overhead pull switch.
TYME	SL 750	125	750	1/2	3 590-2,500	Poly V	1● Bar	—	40	1	—	2 sizes of woodscrew chuck in a set
UK	Cub	125	500-1,000	1/2	4 480-2,000	Poly V	2■ Bars	—	40	1	—	2 sizes of cupchuck in a set
	Avon	140	610-1,200	3/4	4 470-2,000	Poly V	2■ Bars	—	45	2	—	Cub and Avon have swivelling headstocks. Toolrest post available. Stands available.
VEGA	1500 series	380	485-2,440	1	320-3,400	V	Cold rolled steel tubing	—	106-172	2	Yes	Variable speed. Duplicator available
USA	1200	300	275-2,900	1/2	9 275-3,900	V	Cold rolled steel tubing	—	52	2	—	Reversible, two distinct ranges of speed
VIEL CANADA	N/A	255	1,200	1/2	4	V	2○ Tubes	—	—	—	—	Duplicator available. Supplied as a kit without motor or tubes or complete.
WILLIAMS AND HUSSEY USA	Powerlathe	300	1,170	1/2	4 800-3,750	V	CI Machined	—	38	—	Yes	Screw-on centres. Drill chuck adaptor screws to head- or tailstock
WOODFAST	BL 300	420	300	1	4 250-1,300	V	CI Machined	Yes 500 x 134	—	No 2 in tailstock	Yes	Superchuck. Indexing facility
AUSTRALIA	M400 H	305	380	3/4	4 375-2,000	V	CI Machined	—	165	2	Yes	Indexing facility
	MC 900	300	1,000	3/4	370-2,000	V	CI Machined	—	—	2	610	Indexing facility, handwheel brake

All sizes are quoted in metric.

■ – Solid square   ● – Solid round   □ – Tube   CI – Cast iron

4

WORKING BETWEEN CENTRES

Work carried out between centres – spindle turning – needs the addition of two centres; one at the headstock, which serves to centre and drive the workpiece, the other in the tailstock to centre and support the work. Headstock centres can either be screwed to the spindle or turned to a specified Morse taper and inserted into it. The headstock centres are usually referred to as prong centres, since they have a centre point and a number of chisel-like prongs that engage in the timber to provide the drive. These can have two or four chisels, the latter giving the better drive. Some of these are very accurately made with removable/replaceable centres, which greatly add to the life of the tool. They are also available in smaller sizes for the miniaturist, and these usually have extended length to facilitate working close to ends of small turnings (Figs 10, 11).

The centre at the tailstock end, supplied as standard, is often referred to as the dead centre, since it does not revolve with the workpiece. Usually offered as an optional extra is the running (or live) centre. The latter is to be preferred since the dead centre needs lubrication, otherwise there is a danger of burning; lubrication, if overdone, can result in stained work and ruined shirts. The dead centre comes in solid or cup form; with the running centre there is less bearing surface, and usually this type has a replaceable point. Some have a very tiny centrepoint and should this become damaged the centre is useless (Fig 12).

RUNNING CENTRES

The running centre was designed for the worker in metal who prepared the centre of his work by boring with a Slocombe drill.

10 4-prong drive centre

11 Various styles and sizes of centre

This removed the possibility of overheating and reduced wear of both components. It is only in recent years that this particular tool has been added to the woodturner's kit. Previously we had to use grease or oil with the solid centre to prevent burning. This burning was somewhat reduced by the introduction of the ring-type dead centre.

A simple, inexpensive running centre is now available for woodturning and we may well see this becoming standard equipment, rather than an optional extra, with the modern lathe (see centre Fig 12).

Some years ago, Rockwell in the United States produced a running centre, which offered options of style. The actual centre piece was removable giving a choice of solid or cup and also offering a drill pad.

During a visit to the States I picked up an experimental centre which my good friends, the brothers Parker at Coronet, modified. This had both cup and solid centres and in addition a component with a screw end, which was an exact copy of the Coronet spindle ¾×16tpi. To this could be screwed any one of the cone centres the company made at that time. Thus the turner had a number of options for holding work between centres. Cones were sized to hold timber between ¼ and 2in (6 and 50mm). I carried out a further modification to the screw component by drilling and tapping the solid end to receive a ¼in (6mm) threaded bolt. This then offered the

12 Types of tailstock centre

facility of mounting wooden discs in various diameters with a moderate taper. These could be used to support hollowed-out work such as goblets when shaping the outside after the heavy inside work had been completed. This is particularly useful with slender stemmed work.

Between-centre work can also be carried out using a pair of cones or a single cone at the headstock end. These cones, made by Coronet, are threaded ¾in or ⅞in to suit old and new style Coronet lathes. Tapered mandrels in Nos 1, 2 or 3 are available to facilitate the use of cones with any lathe having sleeves of those tapers. A cone running centre is also available which permits the assembly of reducing cones at the tailstock end to match those at the other end. Thus single, halved, or quartered, workpieces can be accepted within the various sized cones and driven with safety.

The Teknatool centre system comes from Latalex Ltd (Fig 13). It has a twin-bearing system which incorporates a taper-roller bearing to take extreme thrust loads five to seven times that of the normal type bearing, plus another bearing which runs behind it for precision alignment and extra stability. The ball-bearing units are completely sealed against dust and grit, and wear elements are further hardened to ensure precision and long life. The system comprises a solid centre, a cup centre, and a mini-centre; the other end of this is threaded to serve as a screwchuck. There is also a cone centre which will accept rounds up to 2in (50mm) diameter, split turnings, squares, or any other uncentred work. The mini-centre is extended, which assists greatly when turning small diameter work.

The main components of the system are made in chrome molybdenum steel on computerised machinery. Woodfast has a beautifully made multi-centre kit (Fig 14). Craft Supplies markets a de luxe system (Fig 15) which incorporates a heavy-duty double-row angular contact bearing ensuring a lifetime of reliability, combined with the unique facility of the removable end piece, on a stub-nose taper mandrel for easy removal. There are four removable fittings (Fig 16); they are a 1in (25mm) solid centre which is fitted as standard, a ¾in (19mm) with a length of ¾in (19mm) which makes for great accessibility when work is very small in diameter, a ring centre for use when there is a danger of splitting or the centre of the wood has been damaged and an

13 Latalex Teknatool centre system

14 Woodfast multicentre kit

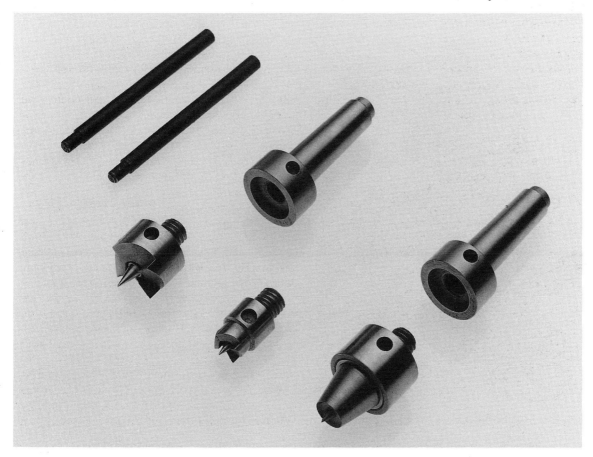

adaptor plate which is fitted with a small bolt and can be used to hold disc supports for bowls and goblets. The system also has a cone centre, with a reducer, which can be used to hold split turnings and small square timber for lace bobbins without having to mark the centre of the work at the start. The reducer will accept timber between ¼ and ½in (6 and 13mm) and the main body ⅝ and 1in (16 and 25mm).

A centre becoming increasingly popular with miniaturists is the lace bobbin drive marketed by Craft Supplies. This is a copy of the wooden ones (see Fig 17) which I have used for many years, de-

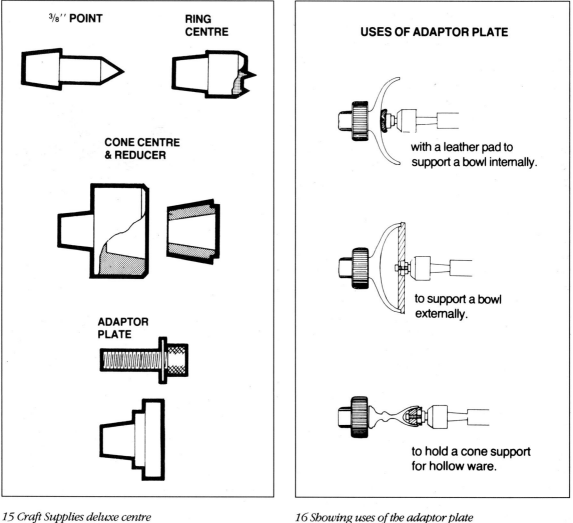

⅜″ POINT

RING CENTRE

CONE CENTRE & REDUCER

ADAPTOR PLATE

USES OF ADAPTOR PLATE

with a leather pad to support a bowl internally.

to support a bowl externally.

to hold a cone support for hollow ware.

15 Craft Supplies deluxe centre

16 Showing uses of the adaptor plate

signed for children to turn small parts. Manufacturers failed to take up my suggestion for this piece with the excuse that the centre-cut truncated-cone shape was difficult to produce. Tyme Machines came up with the answer – cast it and make an insertion of it – I would still like to see one that will drive pieces from ⅛in (3mm) upwards for accommodating very tiny pieces. It is interesting to note that the Coronet Tool Company, when asked to look at this drive, came up with the cone as an alternative (Fig 18).

PREPARATION OF TIMBER FOR TURNING BETWEEN CENTRES

Take a pencil and rule and draw diagonals at both ends of the square timber to find the centres.

If a two prong centre is being used, make two saw cuts, one each side of the centre line, about ⅛in (3mm) apart. These will serve to house the chisel prongs which are slightly offset either side of centre.

If using a four prong centre, two saw cuts along the diagonals will serve to house the chisels.

At the tailstock end, penetration by the centre itself is usually deep enough to accommodate the centre safely. Should this not be the case, an engineer's centre punch can be used.

The practice of tapping the driving fork into the wood with a soft faced hammer or mallet is not to be recommended, particularly in teaching, where the young user may not be aware of the dangers of 'mushrooming' the end of the centre which prevents its perfect insertion in the taper of the headstock spindle.

With the younger beginner it may be as well to remove the corners of the workpiece with the plane before commencing to turn. This will reduce the noise a little and the splintering effect of the first few cuts, and perhaps smooth the introduction of the youngster to turning.

If cones are being used, no preparation of the timber is necessary. Select the size of cone to accommodate the timber safely.

Between-centre work, particularly using timber of small section, needs the use of a lace bobbin drive. Here the timber is accommodated at the headstock end by a tapered mandrel into the end of which has been cut a square pyramidic hole to house square stock comfortably.

17 Lace bobbin drive and Sainsbury's earlier drive

18 Cone centres

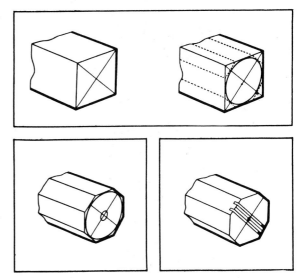

19 Preparation of timber

5

CHUCKS AND FACEPLATES

The earliest development was the faceplate, which could be attached with screws and bolts or by screwing on to the mandrel nose. With lathe development and the use of both ends of the headstock, a proliferation of varying sizes of faceplate appeared. Faceplates as large as 16in (406mm) were provided for the left hand end and upwards of 8in (200mm) on the right. Such large sizes are largely unnecessary, 3 or 4in (75 or 100mm) being perfectly adequate for most work.

Early woodturners had discovered the advantage of the screw and often made up simple woodscrew chucks in wood. Myford in England, provided, in the early forties, left and right hand screw chucks for their ML8 lathe. The early ones had screws brazed in place which made replacement difficult. Harrison on the other hand held the woodscrew in place with a grub screw, making it easily replaceable.

Coronet greatly improved the screw chuck to incorporate a No 14 screw, interchangable for length with facilities for adjusting the length of the screw protruding through the face. The body of the chuck has a threaded centre plug that houses a tongue on to which the slot in the screw fits. This plug is threaded for adjustment to suit the length of screw required; a grub screw locks it in position; another screwed plug secures and centralises the woodscrew. Its underside is countersunk to receive the head of the woodscrew and two small holes on the face, diametrically opposed, permit a spanner to be used to tighten it. A number of woodscrew chucks have been manufactured but none better than this one (Fig 21).

Timber must be prepared carefully before assembling to the screw chuck. The face must be flat with a centre hole drilled of diameter equal to the core size of the screw. If the timber is thin and penetration completely through the block is undesirable, reduce the screw length by adding discs of

20 3 inch (75mm) faceplate

21 Coronet screwchucks with adjustable screws

hardboard or plywood. Make the holes in the discs slightly oversize to accommodate any swelling or 'throw-up' around the hole. If timber of fairly large diameter is being accommodated, cut hardboard discs of smaller size – these will help to support the thinner timber during working. The recessed face on my Harrison screw chuck provides firm support for the timber, even if the screw has 'thrown up' the wood around the hole.

Quite large timber can be set up on the screw chuck. Where the screw is placed in end grain, take care at the commencement of cutting, particularly if the work is badly off centre, to avoid stopping the job by jamming the tool, since this will strip the cut thread. The screw in the Craft Supplies precision combination chuck and in the Glaser chuck is purpose designed (ie not a woodscrew). It has a finely cut knife edge thread on a parallel core. This cuts cleanly into a hole bored in the workpiece and provides a safe hold making for easy and accurate reassembly. Where the woodscrew is used the turner is advised to use the twinfast type, which has a finely cut parallel thread (see page 84).

An economic variation on the standard chuck is shown in the Tyme Machines combination screw chuck (Fig 22). The design offers a 1¼ and a 3in (32 and 75mm) screw chuck using one body. The faceplate, into which a standard woodscrew fits, is attached to the body using two Allen-head screws. An excellent idea, but were I able to influence the company, I would recess the face and use the Craft Supplies type screw. I suggest that these screws should be available in several lengths and have a standard diameter of ⁵⁄₁₆in (7mm)

The Glaser chuck is an excellent example of the work of a thinking man. Jerry did not invent the woodscrew but for his first chuck he invented the woodturner's screw and manufacturers worldwide have copied it. The thread of his screw is parallel and has a finely cut form which enables it to wind neatly and strongly into a pre-drilled hole in the workpiece. The parallelism ensures perfect centrality if work has to be returned to the lathe. In the light of experience, the first chuck, made in steel, was withdrawn after a very successful run and replaced with the one shown in Fig 23. This chuck has a 2in (50mm) diameter body housing a ⅜in (10mm) screw with a ¼in (6mm) core which is held in place with a removable pin, just in case you damage the screw and need to replace it. A reversible tapered collar screws to the body and offers faces of 2½in inch (64mm) and 3½in (89mm). Both faces are recessed to clear any throw-up of timber around the base of the screw, which might create problems during turning. It is a beautifully machined chuck and perfect in use (Figs 24, 25).

22 Tyme Combination screwchuck

23 Glaser screwchuck

24 Glaser screwchuck in 2½in (63mm) mode

25 Glaser screwchuck in 3½in (90mm) mode

CUP CHUCK

Early craftsmen woodturners used the wood chuck to house their partly turned work. This was a simple recess cut in a block of wood of size to fit the outside diameter of the particular job. A hardly perceptible taper permitted the work to be pushed in and held securely to complete the job.

This is an ideal method, particularly for turning plates, dishes and bowls. Smaller versions allowed for holding by cutting a small plinth or spigot on the underside of the dish or bowl.

A number of companies attempted to fulfil this need by the manufacture of the cup chuck. Some earlier versions were disastrous and were withdrawn. Usually having a recess of about 2in (50mm) diameter with a slight inside taper, the present day cup chuck serves to hold timber pre-turned between centres and intended for such work as eggcups and serviette rings, or work first held on a faceplate with a spigot turned on the underside to fit in the chuck. This is a sound method of bowl chucking, where the spigot can be left in the final design or removed to leave a perfectly flat base.

Alternatively the body of the precision combination chuck can be used as a cup chuck of internal measurement 2⅛in (54mm) diameter also the collet/spigot chuck which has an internal measurement of 1⅞in (47mm) diameter. A version is made by Tyme Machines. Here again we have a 'two-size' job, the larger housing a smaller chuck, which is held in place by an Allen-head grub screw (Fig 26).

26 Tyme cup chuck with reducer

CHUCKS

Undoubtedly the greatest step forward in the development of holding devices for the woodturning lathe came with the introduction of chucks with the expanding jaw. Craft Supplies at Millersdale in Derbyshire first introduced this feature in a chuck called the Six-in-one and this was the vehicle that served to prove the idea and the working possibilities. The company was wise inasmuch as it contained not only good listeners but also action men. They were able to use their teaching school and skilled staff to follow through and test suggested changes and modifications. The early chucks were good but not good enough and the precision combination chuck was born into a company woodturning wise. The success of their work in this field has transformed 'The Mill' into the 'Mecca of Woodturners' and people travel from all over the world to meet Mohammed and examine his goods.

27 Precision combination chuck

The precision combination chuck is made on CNC machines and is of such accuracy that all parts are completely interchangeable from one chuck to another (Fig 27). The user can therefore add to his components from time to time as the need arises, or the pocket permits, without any problems of fitting or running. Such accuracy eliminates the problems of centrality which have long plagued the turner when returning work to the lathe for alteration or for further turning to be carried out. The chuck and its components are extremely strong. Quick and easy to use, the chuck has up to ¼in (6mm) adjustment on all the expanding collets. It is streamlined, and there are no parts which project to injure the hand or tool. The design of the chuck and its components is such that the minimum of timber is wasted. Work can be held without any unsightly marks or holes being left on completion; neither does the chuck tend to influence the design. All surfaces can be completed at one setting right up to the polished state.

The basic package comprises the chuck body and collar, centre boss, 3½in (90mm) expanding dovetails jaws, 1in (25mm) pin chuck with pin, 1¾in (45mm) 3-way split ring together with a thin washer, screw, Allen keys and 2 C spanners. This basic kit offers most woodturners adequate solutions to their holding problems. Should the need arise many additional components are available, including nine sizes of expanding dovetail collets, two sizes of 3-way split rings, three sizes of spigot chuck, five sizes of pin chucks, three sizes of collet chuck, three sizes of screw chuck and six sizes of faceplate rings. Also there is a conversion kit for the small size of collet and for the adjustable collets. The chuck can be housed in a very strong metal case with a polystyrene container. The latter can be obtained separately should the turner wish to make his own case.

Chucks are available to suit almost every good quality lathe produced in the world today, but unthreaded bodies can also be obtained.

EXPANDING DOVETAIL COLLET CHUCK MODE

This is the main and most important mode of the precision combination chuck. It comprises a body into which is fitted a centre boss. This boss expands a set of jaws when the chuck collar is screwed up. The jaws, which can be either machined steel or cast, have an angled edge that grips inside a dovetail recess cut in the timber. This provides the safest known method of holding large or small work without the use of screws. Sizes of jaw range between ⅞ and 3¾in (22 and 95mm) which means that any block within the capacity of most woodturning lathes can be accommodated and turned without problems.

Components
Body; screwed collar; centre boss; 3½in (90mm) cast expanding dovetail collets.

Tools
Pair of C spanners

Preparation of the timber
The timber should be cut to round on the bandsaw or have its corners removed. It can then be assembled to:

28 Parts of the expanding collet chuck

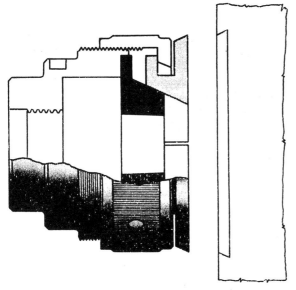

29 Section showing the components in place

30 Fitting the workpiece

a)   a faceplate
b)   a faceplate ring (refer to page 49 for details)
c)   a pin chuck (refer to page 38 for details)

Mount the assembly on the lathe and turn to round; bring the rest across the face of the block and mark a circle with dividers 3½in (90mm) in diameter. Use a parting tool to cut a groove just inside the circle to a depth of ³⁄₁₆in (5mm). Then use a ³⁄₈in (10mm) HSS gouge to make a shallow recess. Use the long corner of a ½in (12mm) skew chisel, on its side, to cut into the corner to form a dovetail recess. Complete this recess to a polished finish; some tiny vee cuts or similar can be cut for decoration. Remove from the lathe, take off the faceplate, or unscrew the screwchuck, or slide off the pin chuck. The underside of the bowl could, of course, be completed at this first turning so that only the inside of the job will have to be turned when remounting to the expanding collet chuck.

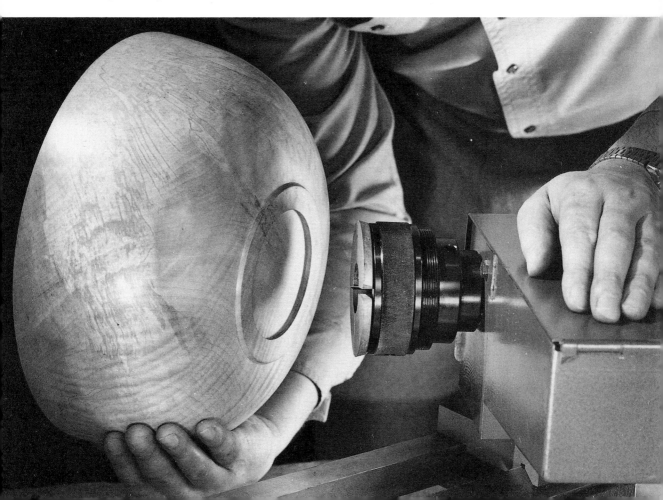

31 Exploded chuck showing the small expander in place in the centre boss

Assembling the expanding collet chuck

Place the chuck complete with its 3½in (90mm) dovetail collets on the lathe. Offer up the recessed block; hold it tightly in place over the collets and tighten the chuck by hand. The collets will expand and fit snugly into the dovetail recess to make a perfect hold. Use the C spanners for the final tightening. There is sufficient movement in the chuck jaws to allow for slight errors of measurement or cutting.

Holding small work (Figs 31, 32)

The ⅞ and 1⅛in (22 and 30mm) collets are provided to permit the holding of smaller and miniature work. A slightly different arrangement has to be made for these. The normal centre boss is too large to be used to expand the jaws, but the chuck can be equipped with a small expander which fits into the Morse taper on the reverse side and is held in place with the washer and screw.

The kit comprises:

⅞ and 1⅛in (22 and 30mm) miniature expanding
  dovetail jaws
small centre boss

Preparation

As for the other jaws except that the boss is reversed in the chuck body.

32 Small jaws in place showing nose of small expander (left – underside of jaws to show recess which accommodates the small expander)

Safety in use

Check for security as the work proceeds, and tighten with the spanners if necessary. Looseness occurs very rarely, but keep listening just in case.

When releasing the chuck to remove the work always hold the work carefully to avoid damage if dropped.

Take care not to drop the chuck when removing it from the lathe.

The chemically black surfaces will protect the chuck from rust, but occasionally wipe the threads with a lightly oiled rag to assist in easy movement and to remove any fouling.

Additional equipment

Apart from the minature collet set previously mentioned, the following jaws are available as optional extras:

machined steel collets (3 jaws)	cast collets (4 jaws)
3in (75mm)	1¾in (45mm)
2¼in (55mm)	2in (50mm)
	2½in (63mm)
	2¾in (70mm)
	3in (75mm)
	3¾in (95mm)

SCREWCHUCK MODE

Designed to hold timber of every description for a wide variety of jobs, the screwchuck is arguably the most versatile piece of work-holding equipment. Formerly screwchucks used a woodscrew, but the screw in this chuck has a parallel core and a fine knifelike thread; it winds easily into the timber giv-

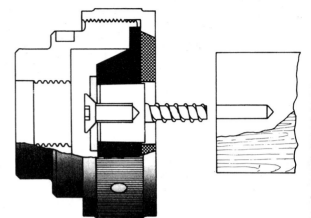

34 Section of chuck and workpiece

ing a very strong fixing. The job can be removed from the chuck and returned to it without loss of centrality or strength.

Components

Body; screwed collar; centre boss; screwchuck with washer and screw; filler ring

Tools

C spanners; Allen keys; drill of size to suit the screw being used

33 Converting to a screwchuck by inserting the screw into the centre boss

Preparation of the timber

Drill a pilot hole at the centre of the workpiece to suit the size of screw being used

> ⅜in (10mm) diameter × ⅞in (22mm) right hand screw – ¼in (6mm) pilot hole
>
> ⁵⁄₁₆in (8mm) diameter × ¾in (20mm) right hand screw – ⁷⁄₃₂in (6mm) pilot hole
>
> ⅜in (10mm) diameter × 1¼in (32mm) left hand screw – ¼in (6mm) pilot hole

Wherever possible provide a flat surface to abut against the face of the chuck to ensure maximum drive.

Assembly

Take the screw best suited to the size of the work – the ¼in (6mm) will be found most useful for smaller pieces. Insert the screw component into the Morse taper of the centre boss – it can only be inserted on the reverse side, and tighten using the washer, screw and Allen key.

Place the chuck body in position on the lathe,

35 Assembling the workpiece

drop in the centre boss, slide over the screwed collar, and tighten by hand finalising with the C spanners. If the filler ring is available this can be positioned inside the screwed collar before assembly. The advantage of using the filler ring is that it will create a space around the screw base which will allow for any throw-up of material around the hole when the timber is threaded on.

Should the screw be overlong, the depth of penetration into the workpiece can be reduced by adding discs of hardboard or plywood. These should have oversize holes, again to allow for any throw-up around the base of the screw.

Cutting procedure

With off-centred work or irregularly shaped work, take care at first cutting to avoid any possibility of stopping the turning piece and stripping the thread.

Safety in use

The thread fitted to your chuck ensures a secure hold, but be sure there is sufficient thread in engagement. Check for security as the work proceeds. With large unevenly-running work, it is an advantage to bring up the running centre for added support at the commencement of cutting. Always drill the hole to the correct size – a larger hole makes for loose work and a smaller one makes hard work of winding on. Although the screws are of special steel they can be strained or even broken.

Additional equipment

The screw itself is supplied as an optional extra in the sizes previously mentioned. Obtain both right hand ones so that you will always have a screw of size to suit the job. The longer left hand screw allows for holding the larger blocks generally associated with outside turning.

Stainless steel screws are also available, these are stronger and will give longer life. There are three sizes:

Right hand
$3/8 \times 7/8$in (10mm × 22mm)
    drill a $1/4$in (6mm) pilot hole
$3/8$in × $1\,1/4$in (10mm × 32mm)
    drill a $1/4$in (6mm) pilot hole

Left hand
$5/16$in (7mm × 20mm)
    drill a $7/32$in (5.5mm pilot hole

The filler ring will also be found useful.

PIN CHUCK MODE

This is designed to hold timber for basic turning particularly of large rough blocks, which will finally be held using one of the other options.

It is also used for holding pre-bored material for turning serviette and other rings, boxes and vases. Partly finished work can be pushed over the pin (if a suitable size of chuck is available) for finishing such work as the undersides of boxes, and also for polishing.

36 Pin mandrel assembly

Components

Chuck body; screwed collar; centre boss; 1in (25mm) pin chuck; pin; washer and screw; filler ring

Tools

C spanners; Allen keys; 1in (25mm) saw tooth cutter or similar

38 Assembling the workpiece

Preparation of the timber

One of the principal uses is the holding of rough blanks for turning, in preparation for second stage assembly to the chuck in its expanding collet, spigot/collet or collet mode. The only preparation then needed is the boring of a hole to receive the pin chuck. This is best carried out using a saw tooth cutter or Forstner bit. The hole must be of exact size and if the Forstner is used it must be moved quickly into the timber to avoid burning the rim. A flatbit could be employed, but care must be taken to engage a fast speed, and to register the brad point of the bit in the timber before switching on. Advance the bit fairly slowly otherwise it may run off centre, particularly

37 Section showing the components of the chuck

when boring end grain. With other applications it is essential to have the pin chuck fit accurately in the work.

Assembly

The centre boss has a No 3 Morse taper housing at its centre and it is into this that the pin chuck slides. It is secured by the washer and screw using the Allen key included with the chuck. Screw the body of the chuck onto the lathe, place the assembled centre boss in place in the body, then screw on the collar, tighten by hand and finally tighten with the C spanner. If the filler ring is available this can be placed inside the collar before tightening; this will speed up the assembly. The ring is a useful, but not essential, part of the equipment.

The chuck can be assembled on the bench if the user prefers. Turn the chuck so that the flat part of the pin is horizontal, then place the tiny pin in the centre of the flat. Next slide on the prepared block, grasp the chuck firmly to prevent rotation, and sharply move the block clockwise to lock it in position. Actually the pin will have moved into its outside position, and during the rotation of the work it will be kept there by centrifugal force. On an outboard assembly this action will be reversed.

Cutting procedure

There are no particular problems here except perhaps when parting off rings or facing the ends of a turning. Do not part completely through, otherwise the tool and the chuck may be damaged. Part almost through, slide the job off, finish on the bench, and return to the chuck for polishing.

To remove the work; secure it to the lathe against rotation and turn it anticlockwise, the pin will resume its centre position and allow the job to slide off quite easily.

Safety in use

An accurately bored hole, the exact size of the pin chuck, is essential – larger holes will negate the action of the tiny pin. Undersize holes will prevent easy assembly. Always check the bit against the pin chuck using a pair of calipers. All the pin bodies have an accuracy close to $2/1000$in as they are machined on highly specialised CNC machines.

Where the assembled job does not completely conceal the tiny pin, the user is advised to place a small piece of Sellotape across the end to secure it against the possibility of flying out during turning; this is particularly important if the turner should be using a pin shorter in length than the flat. The necessity for this procedure will be evident when mounting very narrow pieces. It is, of course, essential to use the correct diameter pin. The pin diameter should be noted. Then, should you lose it, you can replace it with a round nail of that size.

Use as much of the length of the pin chuck as the timber will allow, thus increasing the support. For deep material use the total length, and if the part of the block which abuts against the chuck face is flat this will assist the drive. Check occasionally for security during turning.

Additional equipment

$5/8$, $3/4$, $1½$, $1¾$in (15, 20, 38, 45mm) and 22mm ($7/8$in) pin chucks are available as optional extras, complete with pins.

The filler ring is also available.

COLLAR CHUCK MODE

Designed to hold long pieces of timber for work between centres without the support of the tailstock, this facility permits the turning of hollowed ware such as goblets, eggcups, serviette rings, long and short boxes. It is also suitable for vases and similar work, where some of the turning is carried out at the right hand end of the workpiece.

Precision chuck components needed

Chuck body; screwed collar; centre boss

Tools

C spanners

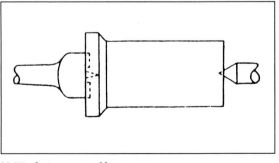

39 Workpiece turned between centres

Preparation of the timber

Select a suitable piece of square section material which should be of sufficient size to give between 2¾ and 3in (70 and 75mm) in diameter, and of sufficient length to leave a waste piece at both ends. Prepare both ends for normal spindle turning between the driving fork and the tailstock centre. Turn to a diameter of 2¾in (70mm) and at this size cut a flange at the left hand end to the sizes as detailed in the illustration. Turn the remainder down to 2½in (63mm), ie the diameter of the inside of the chuck collar. This will permit it to be passed through the collar for assembling.

The end of the flange should be cut square either with the parting tool or the skew chisel, or it can be slightly dished to ensure a firm seating against the reversed centre boss.

Mounting the workpiece on the lathe

Screw the chuck body to the lathe headstock mandrel, and insert the centre boss in the reverse position.

Pass the timber through the collar, and screw up to the body. Tighten by hand and with both chuck spanners.

40 Assembling

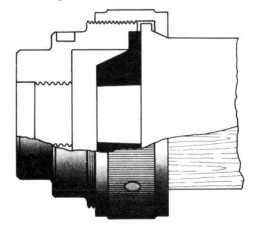

41 Section through the chuck with the workpiece in place

Cutting procedure

When turning eggcups, goblets and similar articles where the heavy cutting takes place at the right hand end, the turner is advised to carry out this work first, while the timber is strong in the mass. Attempting to cut the bowl of a goblet after cutting the stem could prove disastrous.

Care in use

Tighten firmly with the spanners, and check security as the work progresses.

Always listen during turning – a change of note may indicate slackness in the assembly.

Do not work right up to the face of the chuck as this may result in damage to the chuck, the cutting tool, or indeed to the person.

Additional equipment

The filler ring, which can be bought as an extra for use with the chuck in other modes, can be used to reduce the aperture size of the collar to 1⅞in (48mm). It is particularly useful when turning boxes of small diameter and eggcups. The sloping flange can be cut square.

3-WAY SPLIT RING MODE

This is designed to hold fairly long pieces of timber when making goblets, vases, eggcups, long and short boxes, serviette rings and similar work where some of the turning is carried out at the right hand end of the workpiece. The split ring substitutes for the cut flange in the collar chuck mode. This results in a saving of timber.

Components

Chuck body; screwed collar; centre boss and 1¾in (45mm) split ring

Tools

Pair of C spanners

Preparation of the timber

Refer to the section on the collar chuck mode, and prepare the timber for assembly between centres. Turn down to round and to a diameter of 2½in (63mm) throughout the length of the piece. Square up the left hand end of the work with the parting tool or the skew chisel, taking care not to cut too deeply and strike the driving fork with the cutting tool; ⅜in (10mm) from the left hand end cut a groove using the parting tool, ⅜in (10mm) wide and ⅜in (10mm) deep (the diameter will be 1¾in (45mm) which is exactly the same as the internal diameter of the split ring).

Assembly

Insert the split ring into the cut groove, after taking the work from the lathe. Pass the workpiece through the collar so that the sloping face of the split

42 Assembling

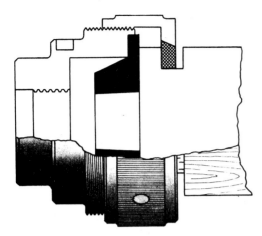

43 Section through the chuck with workpiece in place

ring abuts against the sloping internal face of the collar. Insert the centre boss into the body of the chuck in reverse, offer up the collar with the workpiece and tighten by hand and finally tighten using the C spanners.

Cutting procedure
Exactly as when working in the collar chuck mode.

Safety in use
Check for security as the work proceeds and tighten using the C spanners. Do not work right up to the face of the chuck since this may result in damage to the face of the chuck, the cutting tool or indeed the person.

Additional equipment
Split rings of 1½ and 1¼in (38 and 32mm) bore diameter are available as optional extras. With these, timber of size between 2¼ and 2in (55 and 50mm) diameter can be used. Larger work can be held, but the timber must be turned at the left hand end with a spigot of sufficient length to allow the workpiece to be pushed through the collar so that the split ring can be inserted in the groove. This can be wasteful of timber, and it is suggested that the turner should consider using the expanding collet mode or the spigot mode instead.

SPIGOT COLLET CHUCK MODE

This chuck offers two different methods of holding work and is particularly useful where the finished

work will have a natural edge. A bowl or dish can be completed, outside and inside, without reversing once a dovetail spigot or a longer parallel spigot has been cut. It is also useful for box work and for holding long and narrow ware. The holding spigots can be removed and the base sanded after the turning is completed. Alternatively the spigot can be used as a design feature.

Components
Chuck body; screwed collar and 2in (50mm) spigot jaw

Tools
Pair of C spanners

Preparation of the timber
There are several options:

a) large blocks mounted on the pin chuck can have a 1⅞in (48mm) parallel spigot turned on the end. This turned end will be inserted into the parallel portion of the spigot jaw and held quite firmly when the chuck is tightened.

b) smaller pieces can be turned between centres. Here a 1⅞in (48mm) parallel spigot can be cut about 2in (50mm) in length at one end. If the work is to be 1⅞in (48mm) diameter or less, the timber can be turned to that diameter and pushed into the chuck leaving sufficient length for the work in hand protruding.

c) small box material can be turned between centres and a dovetail spigot cut at each end. This will permit the holding of both the top and bottom without problems of loss of centricity. Partial turning can take place between centres, then the piece can be cut in two to make the top and bottom. The cut spigot fits into the forward part of the jaw, and the inside of the top can be turned at this setting. This is followed by the box itself which can be turned completely, the lid attached, and finished in situ. Finally the spigot can be removed on the sanding table and the base polished. There are several options of procedure here.

d) plates, dishes and platters of various shallow sections can be held using the dovetail spigot, the disc being first prepared by mounting to:
   i) faceplate ring and very short screws.

44 Inserting the spigot/collet jaw

ii) faceplate.
iii) screwchuck with a number of plywood discs to restrict the amount of screw penetration.
iv) hot melt glue used on a wood block attached to a faceplate ring.

Here again the little spigot can be removed after completion of the turning.

Assembly

Assemble the chuck on the bench and then onto the lathe. Insert the prepared spigot or dovetail spigot into the chuck, tighten by hand, and finally with the spanners.

Cutting procedure

Particularly when using the dovetail spigot, make frequent checks to ensure perfect gripping. If the work is offset, take care when starting to cut.

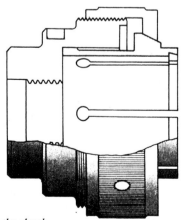
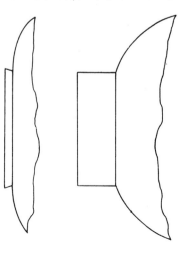

45 Section through the chuck

46 Assembling the partly turned bowl

Safety

DO NOT OVERTIGHTEN THE STEEL COLLET, permanent damage can be caused. The collet is constructed in this slender form to be flexible enough to be contracted easily. Such a construction can be distorted with overtightening. It is suggested that the purchase of a 1¾in (45mm) pin chuck would not only provide a useful accessory, but since it has a 1⅞in (48mm) diameter shaft this could be pushed into the collet after use to assist in maintaining its correct diameter.

ADJUSTABLE COLLET CHUCK MODE

This is similar in its holding system to the collet/spigot chuck, but the jaws are adjustable. They offer a capacity between ¾ and 1½in (20 and 38mm) in two sizes of jaw. The chuck can be used for holding many small items of turnery including: boxes, vases, goblets, eggcups, furniture knobs and pulls, finials and a host of small turning from pre-turned round material, inserted in the pure collet mode.

Components

Body; screwed collar; collet conversion kit comprising a female centre boss and reducing ring

The female centre boss provides a means of closing the collet by the action of its conical form, while the reducing ring closes the screwed ring aperture to ensure a snug fit around the collet when the chuck is tightened. The machined steel collets are spring loaded to give up to ¼in (6mm) adjustment in diameter.

Preparation of the material

Refer to the section on the spigot/collet mode since preparation is exactly the same. Ignore section d) since these jaws would not be used for heavy work.

Assembly

Select the jaws of size to fit the piece of timber. Take the body and insert the female boss. Place the adjustable collet inside the tapered boss, and slip the

reducing ring inside the collar screwing it up to the chuck body. Lightly tighten, then screw the chuck to the lathe. Insert the workpiece, again tighten by hand and at the same time push the timber well into the chuck. Finally use the spanners.

Cutting procedure

Start carefully as always, check periodically, particularly when using the dovetail spigot itself.

Safety in use

No problems with this mode, since the chuck is well made.

Additional

All non-standard parts are optional extras, but it must be remembered that the collet conversion kit has to be used with either set of jaws. These are available in two sizes:

machined steel collets capacity
               ¾in to 1in (20 to 25mm)
machined steel collets capacity
               1¼ to 1½in (32 to 38mm)

47 Components – female centre boss, jaws, reducing ring

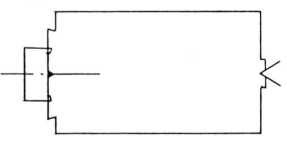

48 Timber prepared between centres

49 Adjustable spigot/collet chuck assembled

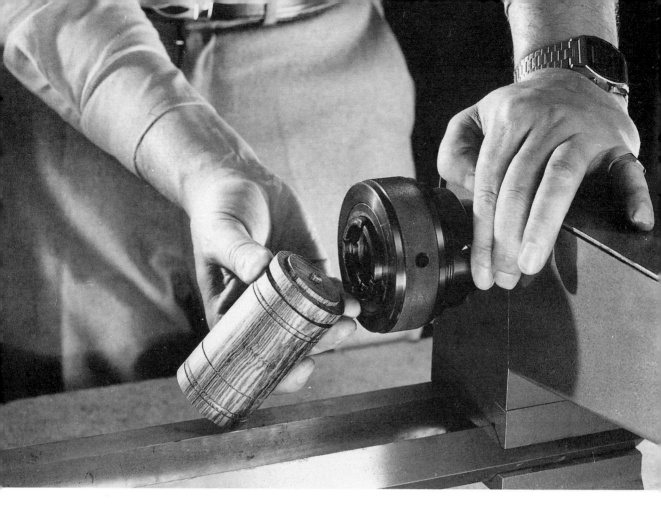

50 Assembling the prepared piece

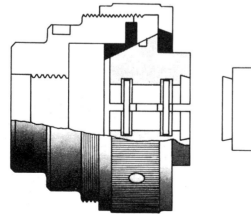

51 Section through the chuck

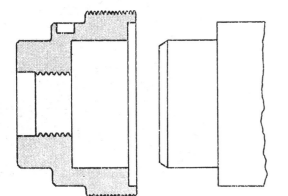

52 Chuck body

CUP CHUCK MODE

The body recess is machined to house accurately the centre boss which acts as expander for the expanding collet chuck and, in the reverse position, houses other components. This recess offers an added bonus as a cup chuck to hold partly turned work by a small spigot.

Preparation of the timber

Timber turned to 2⅛in (53mm) diameter can be pushed into the chuck and, if it is close to an 'interference fit', the work will be held quite securely for turning. Larger blocks can have a small tenon spigot at the end, 1in (25mm) long and 2⅛in (53mm) diameter.

Small work, such as plates, platters and shallow bowls, should have a small boss 2⅞in (73mm) diameter and ⅛in (3mm) deep cut on the underside. This will push into the larger diameter front portion of the body.

53 Section through the body

54 Workpiece fitting into the body

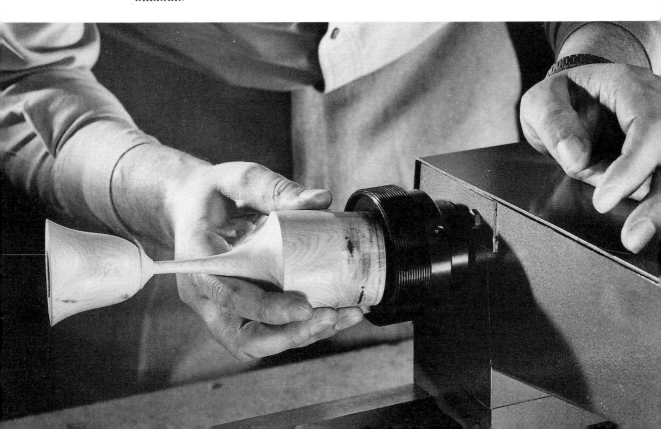

Assembly

Screw the body to the lathe after tapping home the block of wood. It is advisable to carry out this assembly on the bench if hammering is necessary. This will avoid damage to the lathe bearings.

Safety in use

When using cup chucks, always bring the toolrest as close to the work as possible. Should the workpiece move, the rest will prevent it from coming out of the chuck. With thin work, wherever possible bring the toolrest slightly above centre height: this is again a safety measure to prevent flying objects.

FACEPLATE RINGS

These make faceplates unnecessary since they can be used with the combination chuck to hold work at the outset of turning.

The rings have a dovetail recess on the internal diameter of size to match the expanding collets.

55 Faceplate ring assembling

Eight countersunk holes are drilled around the circumference to receive countersunk wood screws for holding the blocks.

These rings are useful where batch work is to be undertaken, but they will probably see their greatest use in the school and college workshop, where often a job cannot be completed at one session and may have to be left over for several weeks.

The initial cost is low in comparison with the cost of faceplates.

Tools needed

Screwdriver and bradawl together with matching expanding collets fitted in the chuck.

Assembly

All rings have eight holes; four will usually be sufficient, but if the block is very large more can be used. Position the ring centrally on the block, pierce

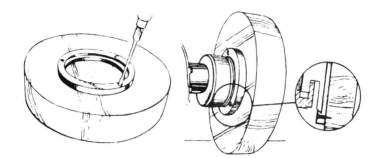

56 Detail of the faceplate ring

through each hole with a bradawl, insert screw and tighten hard.

On the bench, place the assembled expanding collet chuck in position with the jaws inserted into the dovetail recess. Tighten by hand to expand the jaws. Attach the assembly to the lathe and tighten finally using the C spanners.

Safety in use

There are no real problems. Carry out the normal checks as the job proceeds.

Additional equipment

Faceplate rings are an optional extra and are available in five sizes to suit collets of 3¾, 3½, 2¾, 2½, 2, and 1¾in (95, 90, 70, 63, 50 and 45mm)

Timber preparation for other chucks described in the following pages will be similar to that for the precision combination chuck; where there is a departure this is noted in the text.

The 3-jaw accessory for the combination chuck greatly simplifies the holding of small turnings. It fits into the body of the chuck, and is actioned by tightening the chuck collar which bears on the sloping edges of the jaws (Figs 57, 58, 59).

57 3-jaw chuck

58 3-jaw chuck at work

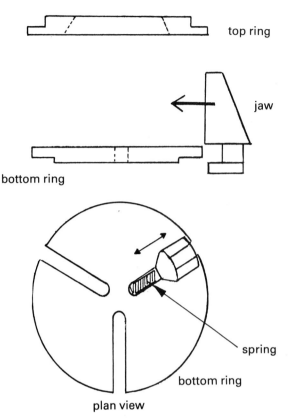

top ring

jaw

bottom ring

spring

bottom ring

plan view

59 Details of the chuck

COLLET/SPIGOT CHUCK

The handy collet chuck was the first of the small chucks and made an excellent vehicle for the launch of improved equipment for holding stock in the lathe. Yes, it had its faults. After the six-in-one came a little known, but excellent chuck, named the spigot chuck. This was designed to hold stock for boxes, introduced the spigot jaw, and also served to hold the popular pin mandrel – the latter two greatly expanding the versatility of the chuck. The spigot chuck has proved to be a winner, and Craft Supplies, always seeking to provide precision and an improved finish, has put the collet and spigot chucks together and produced a good looking and extremely useful chuck (Fig 60) that will accept the spigot/collet jaws of the old spigot chuck and some of the collet/spigot jaws of the precision combination chuck. The chuck has two sizes of spigot, two sizes of expanding collet, two sizes of gripping collet, three sizes of pin chuck as well as two sizes of screwchuck. It has a great advantage in size, being only 2¾in (70mm) in diameter. It is self-centring and work can be removed without loss of centrality.

The spigot collet is made from one piece of steel and is therefore very accurate. Slots in the steel wall give flexibility and allow the collet to be tightened onto the work. It can be used with a small dovetail shaped spigot, to be cut as a feature. These jaws, used with heavier work, will need a longer parallel spigot which can be pushed well into the inner parallel portion.

The centre boss of the chuck will receive the screwchucks, the pin chucks and mini-centre boss from the combination chuck. Two mini-collets are also available in 1 and 1¼in (25 and 31mm) diameter. They must be used with the two centre bosses. It is an ideal chuck for the miniaturist and the turner making small bowls and boxes. The body of the chuck can be used as a simple cup chuck with a capacity of 1⅞in (47mm).

60 Collet/spigot chuck with spigot collet fitted (right – adjustable collet)

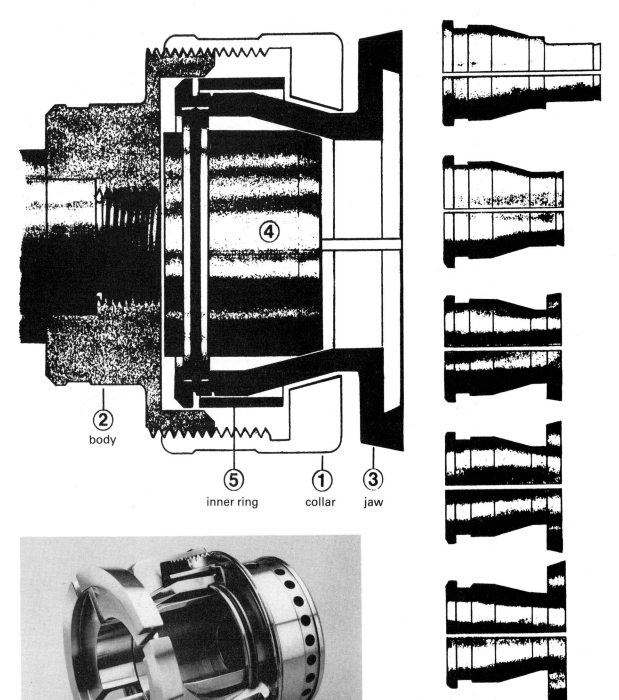

② body

⑤ inner ring

① collar

③ jaw

jaws

62 Sectioned chuck to show detail

MULTISTAR DUPLEX CHUCK

The Multistar chuck has been designed to meet most of the holding problems which the woodturner faces, and it is a most impressive looking piece of equipment. Most parts are bright finish, the machining of the steel and the finish of the jaws compares more than favourably with all the other chuck jaws currently available. The chuck is, at one and the same time, an expanding collet chuck, a collet chuck, a spigot chuck, a screwchuck and a pin mandrel chuck. A universal carrier can also be fitted to carry Morse tapered components. Stripped of its jaws it can be used as a collar chuck with or without the use of a split collar. In addition, the body of the chuck has been drilled around its periphery so that the chuck can be used for indexing. A locking arm is available which can be attached to the lathe. There will be occasions when the turner will need to make his own jaws, and to simplify this a compression ring has been included in the optional accessories list.

The chuck has six sizes of jaw, all of which serve in both expanding and contracting mode. They are machined to grip inside a dovetail-shaped lip on the underside of a bowl or on a spigot of similar shape. Each jaw can also be used as a straight collet.

The chuck consists of a body, the inside of which can be used as a simple chuck, collar, outer ring, expander, inner ring with 'O' ring and jaws. It also has a basal flange which can be inserted into the chuck to give added support for long work placed within the chuck in the collet mode.

In the expanding mode, all the components are needed except the basal ring, but when converted to the spigot/collet mode the outer ring and expander are removed. Details of the jaws are shown in Fig 63 and it will be seen that the three smaller sizes are slightly different in design from the others, while still fulfilling the same function. The smallest sizes will not receive the pin mandrels but will serve as mandrels in themselves expanding into a deep hole without the use of a pin.

Each jaw can be assembled by passing through the collar; in the expanding mode the outer ring will be in place inside the collar. The jaws are equi-spaced by the insertion of an inner ring into a groove inside the rear of the jaws. This ring has an 'O' ring around its periphery to prevent slip; the makers also supply

63 Multistar chuck – large jaws

64 Multistar chuck – small jaws

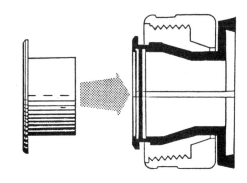

65 Section to show the expanding action

66 Basal ring

*67 Sectioned chuck
   in collet mode*

a rubber band, which helps to support the jaws when assembling. An expander slides inside the inner ring and serves to expand the jaws when the collar is tightened. A clever little feature in the design ensures equi-spaced jaws (so very important), and automatic movement with a springlike action. The body can be screwed to the lathe spindle before final assembly. The jaws move easily into the cut recess in the work, and tightening is effected with a C spanner and tommy bar. A useful addition to these is the orange dip coating at the handle end, a great help if they disappear into a heap of shavings. The jaws grip well without excessive tightening and locate accurately in the recess. The selection of the jaws must relate accurately to the workpiece, large pieces using the small jaws could lead to problems.

When the collet mode is required, the outer ring and expander must be removed from the inside of the chuck (Fig 66). The basal flange can also be inserted. Upon screwing up the chuck the jaws will close in the normal manner of the collet and tightly

over a spigot, offering splendid holding for boxes and similar work (Fig 67). Alternatively, the workpiece can be placed within the jaws with the basal flange giving extra support when holding large work which has been prepared with a long spigot at the base, or prepared rounds of exactly the same size as the collet.

The collets also receive the pin mandrels, screwchuck and universal carrier. Apart from the three smaller sizes, the pin mandrels, in five sizes, fit into the four larger jaws (Fig 68). They are chemically blackened, unlike the rest of the chuck and its components which are of bright steel. Hole boring for the pin mandrels, particularly in softwood, must be extremely accurate when assembling rough blanks to the lathe for shaping the outside of a bowl. The recess for reversal onto the expanding jaws must also be accurately cut. The screwchuck has been redesigned (Figs 69, 70, 71) and not only uses the standard screw supplied but also has an adaptor for smaller diameter standard wood screws of the

68 Pin mandrels

69 Screwchuck

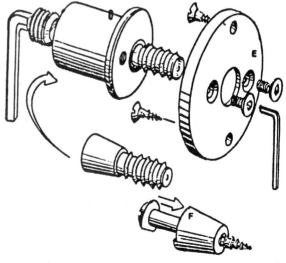

70 Multistar Variform screwchuck detail

*71 Variform screw-
chuck exploded*

72 Chuck with faceplate rings

parallel-sided variety; the large screw is often too large for small jobs, and this is a useful addition. The screwchuck is fitted with a flange giving extra support for larger pieces; this can also be used to reduce the length of the screw in use. Screws are available both right and left hand in ¼, ⅜ and ⁷⁄₁₆in (6, 10 and 11mm) sizes. The left hand thread is only available in ⁷⁄₁₆in (11mm) size. The wood screw is held in place with a powerful screw threaded into the rear of the body, and a small pin at the side prevents the chuck from spinning in the jaws should the user have failed to tighten sufficiently.

The three larger sizes of jaw can be matched to rings that eliminate the need for faceplates, the ring being undercut to receive the dovetail expanding jaws and drilled for screw fixing to the rough block (Fig 72).

The chuck can also use a split ring in conjunction with a filling piece for the assembly of long timber in making of eggcups, serviette rings and boxes, and for any work where the tailstock cannot be used as a support (Figs 73,74,75). See page 42 for the preparation of timber using the split collar chuck.

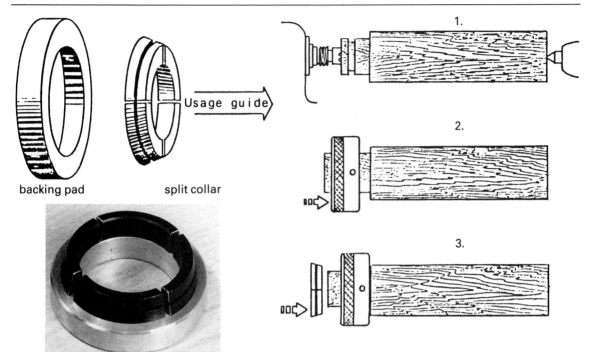

backing pad   split collar

Usage guide

1.

2.

3.

73 Split collar mode – timber preparation and fitting

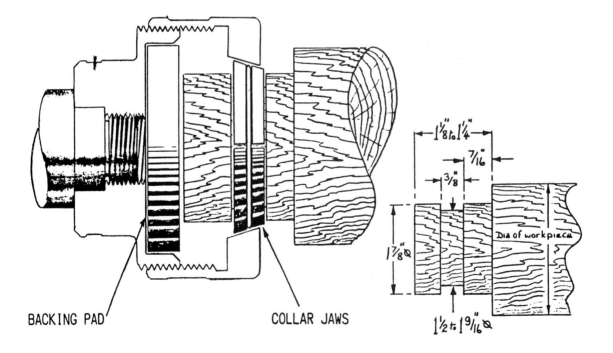

BACKING PAD   COLLAR JAWS

74 Split collar mode – timber measurements

75 Sectioned chuck to show split collar in use

Accessory collet

This is recommended for heavy duty applications and will be found very useful for mounting the pin mandrels and the variform screwchuck. Turners who use wooden mandrels similar to those shown on page 147 will want to use this collet instead of the normal chuck jaws. This will also be so when turning spigot mounted work. Only the body and collar of the chuck are needed (Figs 76, 77. 78).

An index bar, which can be attached to the lathe and left as a permanent fitting, serves to lock the turning in any one of 24 positions using the holes drilled around the periphery of the chuck body. I have used this in conjunction with the router to carve bowls, and many other applications can be devised. The makers suggest that the indexing pin should always be on line with the centre of the chuck (see Fig 79).

76 Accessory collet

77 Accessory collet assembled

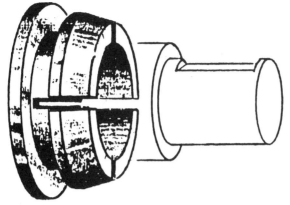

78 Detail of the accessory collet

79 Indexing arm attached to the rear of the Graduate lathe – pin located in the chuck

MULTISTAR EXPANDING BLADE MANDREL

Problems often arise when using the pin mandrel, particularly if the timber is very soft or the hole has been bored slightly oversize. The pin, driven by centrifugal force, may fail to hold the work securely. The expanding blade mandrel is a unique solution to this problem (Fig 80).

It consists of a body which can be located in any one of the four larger Multistar chuck jaws. A barrel is screwed and locked to the body and, through the action of an operating ring and plunger, four jaws hinged at the front of the barrel can be expanded. The barrel is tapered at the rear to provide additional support when articles with a deeply bored hole are being turned. The blades expand about 1/8in (3mm) – which should be sufficient to make up for any slight inaccuracies in boring. Work can be mounted far more quickly, with no pin to lose in the shavings. The mandrel can be further adjusted during working and the blades, retracting like the fletches of an arrow, make for instant and easy removal of the workpiece. Turners of wet timber, which can change shape and distort during turning, will appreciate this.

To use the mandrel, screw the Multistar chuck to the lathe spindle, selecting one of the four larger sizes of jaw with the chuck in the compression mode. It is also advisable to insert the basal flange, to give added support to the expanding blade mandrel which is inserted into the collet jaws. Alternatively, the heavy duty collet could be used. Insert it fully into the rear of the chuck body with the anti-rotation pin located between any two jaw segments. Before fully tightening, check for running perfection.

Bore a 1in (25mm) hole in the workpiece to the required depth (this will vary depending on the type of workpiece being held). The mandrel tolerance is the same as the pin chuck – at 1in (25mm) diameter minus $3/_{1,000}$in (.075mm). Always bore the hole as deep as the work will allow to avoid undue strain on the hinge pins. Load the bored piece, and while pressing firmly in place, tighten by rotating the operating ring with the pin spanner. The jaws must expand fully into the hole – one revolution of the ring brings about full expansion – so do not try to overtighten. The mandrel may require cleaning occasionally; either dip it fully into a good cleaning fluid or, alternatively, strip it by driving out the locking pin with a fine drift and unscrewing the rear body from the barrel.

80 Expanding blade mandrel

81 Woodfast Superchuck exploded

WOODFAST CHUCK

Another concept is the super chuck which has a body that can serve as a faceplate and is drilled accordingly (Fig 81). A screw, threaded at both ends, fits into the centre of the plate, and to this is attached a centre boss which in turn serves to expand a set of three jaws. The jaws are held by an endless spring located in an annular groove around the circumference. They fit into an undercut recess in the bowl blank, and the simple action of tightening the centre boss expands the jaws to hold the blank securely. The jaws expand equally and centre the work without problems should the finished article have to be returned to the lathe for any reason. The recess is made with a special cutter included with the chuck. Two sizes of chuck 2 and 3in (50 and 75mm) are able to fit most lathes, worldwide.

Preparing the workpiece

Plane one face of the workpiece for good backplate mounting. Find the centre, and clamp the block to the drill press table. The block must be firmly held and no attempt should be made to drill with the workpiece held in the hand. Set the drill press at a slow speed. Fit the purpose designed cutter in the drill chuck and tighten firmly. Switch on and advance the drill very carefully until it cuts fully. Drill to 5/16in (8mm) depth. Release from the drill press; remove any waste from the block (Fig 82).

Take the backplate, insert the threaded stud and tighten, using the little box spanner and tommy wrench supplied. Place the chuck jaw assembly in position and secure it by screwing in the expander (also called a clamp) (Figs 83, 84, 85, 86).

Insert the super chuck into the recess in the block, apply pressure, and turn the chuck clockwise until it seats firmly.

82 *Boring the recess for the jaws*

83 *Placing the expander in position*

84 Body screw in position –
   expanding jaw offered up

85 Complete assembly screwed to the
   lathe before attaching block

86 Alternatively attaching the block
   to the chuck at the bench

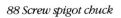

87 Converted to a screwchuck

88 Screw spigot chuck

89 Screw cup chuck

The recess could be cut using the cutter mounted in the tailstock drill chuck, but care must be taken to run the lathe at the lowest speed; the tailstock must be locked in position before switching on the machine. Again, advance the cutter carefully until location is positively made. Large and offset pieces should be supported using the tailstock whenever possible.

To remove the completed job, lock the lathe spindle and turn the job anticlockwise, while pressing firmly against the backplate.

The chuck can also be converted to a screwchuck by placing the threaded screw point in the centre hole of the backplate and tightening with the wrench (Fig 87).

Prepare the job for mounting by drilling a $^{15}/_{64}$in (6mm) hole in the centre and threading the work onto the screwchuck. There are many applications where this will be found useful.

This chuck can also be fitted up as a screw spigot chuck (Fig 88) by adding a spigot with a special thread that cuts into a hole in the workpiece. By screwing up tightly against the backplate, a very positive and trouble-free mounting is made. If the work has to be taken off and later returned to the lathe no problem of centrality arises. Some users of pin chucks have problems with jamming in hardwood and slipping with slightly oversize bores, particularly in softwood; such problems do not arise with this chuck.

The screw spigot chuck can also be obtained as a separate unit to fit many different lathes.

The reverse of the screw spigot is seen in the screw cup chuck (Fig 89). Again, the cutting type thread is used. A spigot is cut on the workpiece which is then screwed into the chuck. Very large pieces can be mounted and, if screwed hard against the flange of the chuck, will be more stable and vibration will be reduced. The traditional cup chuck often created problems of security and offset running if tools were applied incorrectly – problems are largely eliminated with the screw cup chuck. With this chuck too, the workpiece can be removed and returned later without loss of centrality, and the screw cup can be obtained to fit into the super chuck or as a separate unit threaded to fit your lathe. The spigot, 1¼in diameter by 1in long (32 by 25mm), is turned by mounting the workpiece between centres. A small chamfer at the end will help to start the thread cutting at the point of entry of the workpiece into the chuck.

All the chucks are very accurately made for long life and trouble-free working.

THE MASTERCHUCK

This has been designed as a multi-purpose chuck capable of many different functions (Figs 90, 91, 92). The chuck will not only grip the timber within a recess but also on the outside of a spigot. At the same time it serves as a base for mounting other accessories. One useful feature, not provided by any other chuck, is the possibility for the turner to make his own jaws in wood to meet specific design problems. These can be in many shapes and sizes. Plastics could also be used in jaw making. The chuck, which is extremely well machined, comprises a body threaded internally to suit the lathe spindle and externally to receive the outer ring and the locking ring. A centre bolt located in the body secures the nose cone which in turn operates the four chuck jaws.

90 Masterchuck

91 Recess cut to receive the expanding jaws

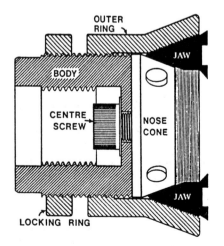

92 Section of the chuck to show detail

The user, when first receiving the chuck, is advised to take it apart carefully to familiarise himself with its operation as it is quite different from the majority of chucks of the expanding type. Remove the locking ring from the back and turn the outer ring to open and close the jaws, which will be seen to remain with their front faces flat and flush with each other.

Take the chuck apart by adjusting the jaws so that they are at the midpoint of their travel. Place the chuck face down on the bench, and loosen the centre bolt (by one turn) through the rear of the chuck body, using the hexagonal wrench. Pick up the chuck, hold the outer ring and the jaws and unscrew the body by one or two turns, which will free the jaws allowing them to be removed. The body can then be taken out through the outer ring. Unscrewing the centre bolt will separate the cone from the body

To reassemble the chuck, first bolt the nose cone and body together so that the boss can turn easily. Screw on the outer ring from behind and position it so that the nose cone is about ¼in (6mm) behind the front edge of the ring. The jaws are numbered 1 to 4 clockwise, and they should be put back in this order. The driving pins in the nose cone fit into the slots in the rear of the jaws. Place the jaws in position so that they are flush with one another. Hold the chuck face up with a finger across the jaws to prevent them turning. Check that the jaws are flush by sighting across them and use the other hand to screw the body into place. The nose cone will be pushed upwards so that it wedges the jaws slightly apart, seating them firmly into the threads in the outer ring. Looking carefully, you will note that the jaws move apart until they are fully seated at which point the body will turn no further. The jaws should be flush with each other without any slack. Correct by unscrewing if there is any doubt. Unscrew the body approximately one twelfth of a turn to give a working clearance. Tighten the centre bolt.

Open and close the chuck to see that it operates smoothly – there should not be more than 1/32in (.8mm) of radial movement in any jaw. Any excess movement will result in loss of rigidity, and will lead to inaccuracies. An excessive working clearance means that only a small portion of thread will be in use, and the chuck could be dangerous when in the expanding mode – it will always be safe in the compression mode because the jaws are thrust into the threads by the gripping forces. Once the jaws have been set up there will be little need to remove them again, even when assembling extension jaws.

If you cannot fathom how the chuck works, assemble it loosely leaving out one jaw so that you can look into the mechanism.

Using the chuck in the expanding mode

Prepare the timber as described on page 33. The locking ring is not really needed here. Screw the chuck to the lathe, place the workpiece over the jaws making sure that they are all in engagement, hold firmly, and tighten by hand. With the lathe switched off, spin the work to make sure, from the area round the jaws, that the workpiece is running true. If the assembly is inaccurate, slacken, push the workpiece hard against the jaws and tighten. Finally use the spanner to tighten fully. Give the assembly a good tug to make sure.

93 Expanding jaw detail

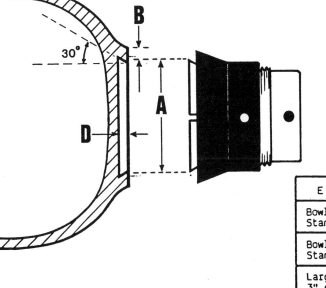

E X A M P L E S	A	B	D
Bowl 6" x 2" Standard steel jaws	2,3/4"	3/8" min.	1/8"
Bowl 10" x 3" Standard steel jaws	2,3/4"	1/2" min.	1/8"
Large bowl 14" x 4" 3" extension jaws	3,5/8"	3/4" min.	3/16"
Small bowl 4" x 3" 1,1/4" ext. jaws	1,1/2"	3/16" min.	1/16" min.

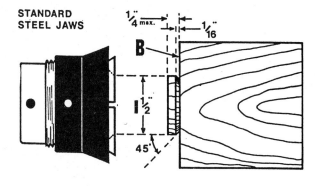

STANDARD
STEEL JAWS

$\frac{1}{4}$" max.

$\frac{1}{16}$"

B

$1\frac{1}{2}$"

45°

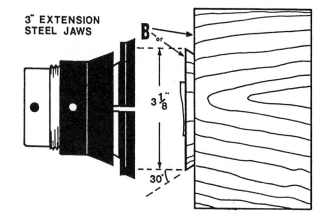

3" EXTENSION
STEEL JAWS

B or

$3\frac{1}{8}$"

30°

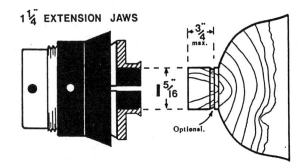

$1\frac{1}{4}$" EXTENSION JAWS

$\frac{3}{4}$" max.

$\frac{5}{16}$"

Optional.

94 Compression mode

Using the chuck in the compression mode

Prepare the timber as outlined on page 43 with the spigot cut as detailed in Fig 94. The face at B should be flat or slightly concave to allow the blank to butt up hard against the jaws. Any slight movement can be eliminated by screwing the locking ring against the outer ring to hold it solidly to the body. The centre bolt must be extra tight when the chuck is used in this mode. When tightening the jaws onto the workpiece spigot, the locking ring should be loose. Use the two C spanners to tighten the chuck then screw up the locking ring, again using the spanners. Check for true running before starting up, and give the job a good tug to check security.

Should the centre bolt not be sufficiently tight, the chuck may suddenly become loose during the tightening process.

The chuck can be used without the locking ring, but the working clearance must be reduced to zero. This method will give more accurate running. Hold the workpiece in the vice, spigot upwards. With the centre bolt tightened, place the chuck over the spigot; use the spanners to tighten the chuck while holding down firmly. With the chuck tightened, loosen the centre bolt and use the small pin spanner to turn the body clockwise into the chuck until it is tight. Re-tighten the bolt. This action reduces the clearance to zero. The working clearance must be restored in order to remove the completed work.

Large cylinders may need extra support for rigidity. This can be done by cutting a large washer from plywood (Fig 97), or other suitable material, and fitting it between the front edge of the outer ring and the rear face of the workpiece. Choose a ring slightly thicker than the gap between the face of the workpiece and the outer ring. On the other hand, a set of large 'bolt-on' steel jaws are available that will eliminate the problem. Probably, for a turner constantly working on large pieces, this will be the answer.

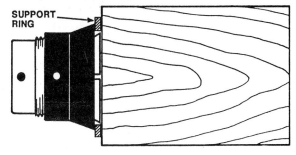

(top) 95 Extension jaws

(centre) 96 Extension jaws

(right) 97 Plywood ring inserted to give greater rigidity

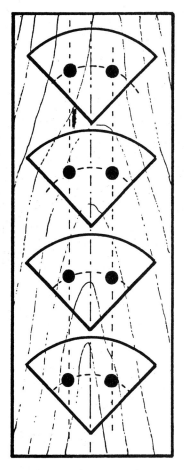

98 Making wooden jaws from a plank of timber

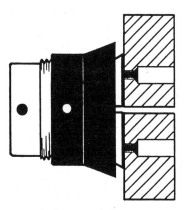

99a Block screwed direct to the jaws

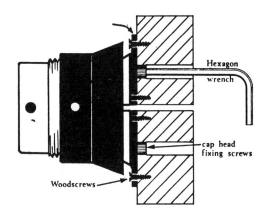

99b Block screwed to steel mounting plates

100 Wooden spigot jaws

101 Another style of jaw

The Masterchuck has been designed so that jaws
of wood or plastic can be turned to shape while
mounted on the chuck (Figs 98, 99, 100, 101, 102).
The facility for locking the jaws without clearance
makes this possible. The hardwood blocks for the
jaws are drilled to take high tensile screws which
screw into the front faces of the standard jaws. Alternatively, jaws can be made in various hard plastics or
good quality plywood. The jaws can be made by cutting a previously turned disc or from a length of
timber with the grain running as in Fig 98. The holes
are $^{3}/_{16}$in (5mm) diameter and in the diagram the
centre lines are $^{545}/_{1,000}$in (14mm) apart and the radius
for the hole centres is $1^{1}/_{20}$in (26.6mm). The turner
may care to make a template for the accurate placement of these holes using thin aluminium sheet.
Mark out and drill them four at a time. Countersink
or counterbore the holes to sink the screws well
below the surface of the jaws.

The jaw blanks can be fitted directly to the standard jaws using the $^{3}/_{16}$in BSF screws, which must be
sunk so as to give clearance for the cutting tools
when the jaws are being shaped. Set up the jaws as
previously detailed and make sure that the wood
jaws will close fully when tightened. Mark the jaws 1
to 4, and attach them to the correspondingly numbered steel jaws of the chuck. Turn the jaws to shape,
and be careful not to to touch any steel parts with the
turning tools (see Fig 101).

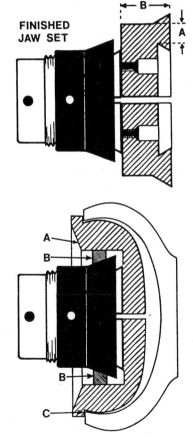

FINISHED
JAW SET

*102 Wooden expanding jaws. Wooden jaws which grip
on the inside and partly enclose the chuck.*

103 Steel mounting plate

104 Screwchuck mode

Steel mounting plates are available to simplify this work (Fig 103). The jaws can be screwed to the plate and the plate to the chuck jaws. The holes in the wood jaws can be bored completely through in this case.

The plate can be used as a template when drilling the holes in the jaw blanks instead of the homemade template suggested previously.

The grip of the jaws can be much improved by undercutting them to a dovetail shape. Straight jaws require great accuracy, and even if they are needed to be straight, they ought to have a slight inward taper (see Fig 102). Ensure that the wood is strong enough, and look critically at the distance 'A'. Have as little jaw overhang as possible since the working leverage at the gripping point will always be considerable. Rigidity problems will arise if the overhang is considerable – with consequent vibration and poor finish.

In Fig 102 a bowl is gripped on the inside by wooden jaws, thus there is little or no overhang. With jaws of this kind clearance must be allowed for the C spanners (see A), also notice the support blocks that have been glued to the inside of the jaws B. A small shoulder at C gives a location and support for the bowl.

The Masterchuck has a screwchuck (Fig 104) which can be set up by removing the centre bolt and replacing it with the machined centre screw. There is no need to disturb the chuck assembly to do this. Make a final check for security and to make sure that in no way has the working clearance been altered.

To prepare the workpiece, drill a ¼in (6mm) pilot hole for the screw in the centre. The length of screw can be adjusted by advancing the jaws of the chuck. Screw the workpiece in place, and be sure that it comes up hard against the jaw faces. Tightening the jaws will bring them even harder against the work.

The pin chuck is undoubtedly the best of its kind. One problem with those that have gone before has been the pin, because it becomes easily lost in the shavings but also because of its small diameter. Unless the hole, particularly in softer woods, is very accurately bored, the workpiece can easily work loose. The pin chuck for the Masterchuck solves both problems (Fig 105). Instead of a flat to house and action the pin, the designer has machined an offset housing into which a spring loaded pin can be pushed and

105 Pin chuck with adaptor and plate

106 Pin chuck fixed to the body

held in place. The pin chuck can be fitted direct to the jaws without dismantling the chuck. An adaptor bush is needed for this. Alternatively, it can be bolted direct to the body to give less overhang (Figs 106, 107). No bush is needed in this mode but the chuck has, of course, to be taken apart – unless you can afford to buy a separate body. Two sizes of pin chuck are available – 1 and 1½in (25 and 38mm) – both need the adaptor bush.

107 Pin chuck attachment detail

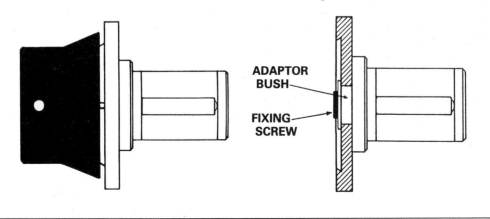

ADAPTOR
BUSH

FIXING
SCREW

108 Direct loading faceplate

Another accessory is the direct loading faceplate (Fig 108) which functions as a simple faceplate, being bored for wood screws, but it also enables direct fitting of both pin chucks and also the new style of screwchuck, to the jaws of the Masterchuck.

The screwchucks can only be used when mounted to the faceplate, (Figs 109, 110). The adaptor bush is not required. These high strength screws have a deep parallel shank thread form for good gripping power and accurate reassembly of the workpiece. Two sizes – ½ and ¾in (12 and 20mm) – come with an Allen key and two fixing screws. The ⁵⁄₁₆in (8mm) screwchuck cannot be used with the faceplate.

Screws can be obtained with slots instead of hexagonal sockets for use when fixing extension jaws; also slotted head screws are available for the direct fixing of self-made wooden jaws to the chuck.

109 Screw and faceplate assembly

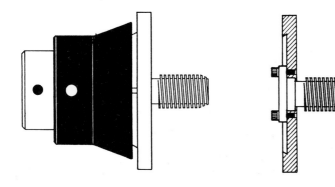

110 Screwchuck detail

SCROLL CHUCK

Many woodturners, and particularly those turning for a living, use the 3- and 4-jaw chucks to hold bowls, boxes and similar work. These are designed for the metalworking lathe with jaws shaped to hold round bar. They tend to mark the wood, and are very large and cumbersome; for safety in working a guard should be fitted. Latalex at Henderson in New Zealand are specialist makers of lathe equipment. They have been producing chucks for some time

and their Multi-chuck II detailed on page 80 has been well researched. The Nova scroll chuck is undoubtedly a major step forward since it uses the scroll method of moving the jaws which gives greater jaw movement. It eliminates the problem inherent in some chucks, of too little expansion which results in a need for great accuracy in sizing the spigot or dovetail recess. The Nova has been developed, using a computer-aided design system, with production controlled by computerised machining technology. A different scroll design to

111 Teknatool screwchuck detail

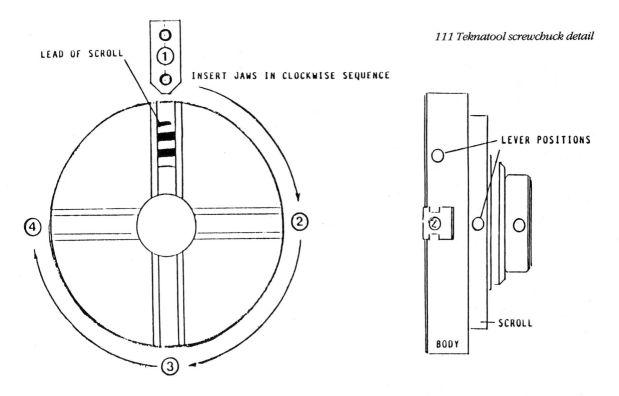

112 Teknatool scroll chuck

113 Teknatool scroll chuck holding square stock

that used in the engineer's chuck has enabled Latalex to make a very compact, small chuck, with only a small overhang; totally suitable for woodturning. The jaws are of steel. The 50mm (2in) is supplied as standard, and others are available. They can be added to the jaw slides, and the jaw action is designed to operate fully within the body section, thus eliminating much of the danger to the hand, ever present in the engineer's chuck. The jaws are shaped to hold in either dovetail or spigot mode. A wood screw called the Woodworm can be inserted and held in place by the jaws, and the screw can also be adjusted for length within its own body. Tool houses stocking this chuck will also be pleased with the universal insert system that will enable the chuck to be universally adapted to a wide variety of lathes. My test chuck was supplied with a Coronet thread, but the company also sent an insert which could be threaded to suit any lathe. For the man working both inboard and outboard, a left hand insert can be used, but a locking device must also be added otherwise the chuck could come unscrewed.

Perhaps the greatest advantage in this chuck is the scroll operation which permits instant change from expanding to contracting mode with no adjustments or extra fittings to be added. At the same time any size of spigot or recess can be used between the maximum and minimum range of the jaw movement. With the add-on jaws removed the jaw slides can be used to grip very small pieces. The grip is extremely powerful, and the contact area of the jaws is considerable, eliminating any marking of the work.

Chuck operation

Two levers are provided for the adjustment of the scroll and chuck body, but where the lathe spindle can be locked the chuck can be activated using one lever. One lever is located in the chuck body, the other in the scroll. Hold the chuck body lever while rotating the other lever in the scroll ring to activate jaw movement. Do not overtighten. This would result in damage to the work or even in bent levers.

The jaw slides are numbered 1 to 4 and they must be inserted in that order. To reset the jaws, rotate the scroll so that the lead of the scroll (a thin wedgelike shape) appears in the opening of any of the slideways. Insert No 1 jaw slide, and rotate the scroll in a clockwise direction (chuck facing you) until the lead of the scroll reaches the next slideway. Engage No 2

jaw with the lead of the scroll. Follow the same procedure with jaws 3 and 4; 50mm (2in) jaws can be removed from the slides by unscrewing the retaining screws with a 4mm (5/32in) Allen key.

The screw chuck, called the woodworm, follows the now well accepted pattern of parallel core and a thin thread form giving excellent gripping power with little likelihood of the work becoming loose.

To use the screw, first place it in the steel insert supplied with the chuck, and lock it in place with the grub screw using the 4mm (5/32in) Allen key, making sure that the grub screw will locate against the flat on the screw shaft. The 50mm (2in) jaws must be fitted before placing the woodworm assembly into the chuck. Make sure that the insert is seated behind and against the 50mm (2in) jaws – this will prevent any tendency for the insert to creep forward when in use. The front face of the jaws has been machined to provide a backing surface, giving accurate location of workpieces. The screw depth can be adjusted by varying the distance the screw shaft is set into the insert – the maximum distance is 25mm (1in) approximately.

The 9.5mm (3/8in) thread requires a drilled hole 6.5mm (1/4in). For ease of removal a little wax applied to the screw will help. If additional purchase is required to screw on the workpiece, use a small adjustable spanner or chain wrench. Take care not to damage the thread when handling.

In the dovetail mode, recesses of between 50 and 75mm (2 and 3in) by 1.5 to 3mm (1/16 to 1/8in) depth can be used depending on the diameter and thickness of the workpiece. Very large pieces will need greater depth of recess. The cutting of the recess is described elsewhere.

In spigot mode, the 50mm (2in) jaws will grip a round spigot between 45 and 56mm (1 3/4 and 2 5/8in). Squares of between 40 and 50mm (1 5/8 and 2in) can be gripped. With the jaws removed the slides will grip small work up to 5mm (1/4in) in diameter.

If the chuck should need cleaning at any time, and if the wood dust build-up is heavy, the chuck may need to be completely dismantled. This can be done using expanding circlip pliers to remove the circlip securing the scroll. The scroll can then be removed and also the jaws. Carefully clean the jaws with a good cleaning fluid, wipe clean, and lightly oil to assist in the reassembly and smooth operation of the

114 Raffan chuck

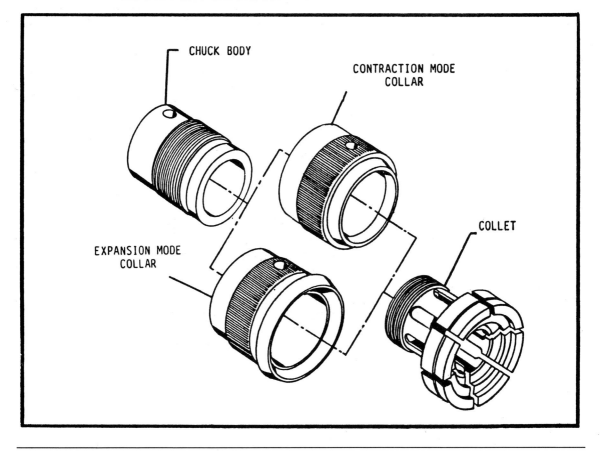

CHUCK BODY

CONTRACTION MODE
COLLAR

COLLET

EXPANSION MODE
COLLAR

chuck. Do not over-oil as this will aggravate the build-up of wood dust. Replace the scroll, secure with the circlip, and reset the jaws as previously described.

When mounting the chuck on the lathe make sure that it registers against the headstock spindle shoulder without interference from dirt or shavings; this will ensure perfect centrality when running.

The chuck inspires great confidence in the user, and its simplicity in setting up is a time saver. The strength inherent in the design and the materials should ensure a lifetime of troublefree use. Other components will appear, also plates to facilitate the addition of wooden jaws.

THE RAFFAN CHUCK

This is a new concept in spigot chuck design (Figs 114, 115) allowing a wide variety of work to be completed in two stages.

Several features make the Raffan chuck more flexible to use than other collet chucks:
a) the collar, which tightens the collet, is mounted on the body before the collet. This permits the use of collets larger than the chuck body or collar, whereas in most chucks the collet size is partly dictated by the size of the body.
b) the collet has a long narrow stem which allows

great flexibility – far more than is available in the popular but wider, split cylinder. This makes the chuck much easier to adjust than others while allowing for a much wider margin of error in sizing than is normal for chucks of this type.
c) the collet is stepped internally to accept a range of sizes.
d) there are two collars which can be wound against the collet – one for expansion, the other for contraction.

How it works

To mount the wood in the chuck, first screw a collar onto the chuck body anticlockwise, choosing either the expanding or contracting mode.

Screw the collet into the body clockwise until it meets the collar.

Lock the lathe spindle to prevent the chuck from rotating, and hold the wood hard up to the chuck to press against the collar. Tighten, using the wrench provided, when the collet will expand (or contract).

The work can be removed from the chuck by locking the lathe spindle and rotating the collar anticlockwise, using the wrench if necessary.

The spigot will grip on as little as 1mm ($1/16$in) but 4mm ($5/32$in) of tenon is suggested as the most suitable. Raffan uses two thicknesses of cotton sheet to protect the wood from the metal.

115 Raffan chuck – another view

116 Dennis Stewart nut chuck

THE NUT CHUCK (Fig 116)

Dennis Stewart has a very effective method of supporting end-grain turnings, especially deep vessels. A tenon is turned on the bottom of the workpiece which is mounted between centres. He then uses a nut chuck which has, at one end, tapered threads on the inside which cut into and compress the tenon, gripping it quite securely. The other end of the nut is threaded internally to fit your lathe. It is similar to the Woodfast cup chuck.

117 Teknatool Multi-chuck II

THE TEKNATOOL MULTI-CHUCK II (Fig 117)

This chuck comes from New Zealand and is a precision product. It comprises a singularly slim body housing the jaws which are both expanding and spigot style, in sizes 2 and 3in (50 and 75mm). The action of the chuck is similar to others having a centre boss for the expanding mode and using the outer ring in the compression mode. It can also be fitted with a screwchuck; the screw is double ended offering two sizes for different wood blanks. The body can serve as a 4in (100mm) faceplate.

A number of accessories are available including a 1in (25mm) expanding/collet jaw and a 4in (100mm) expanding jaw for larger work. Faceplates are also available in both right and left hand versions to mount extra sets of collets.

A woodworm lefthand screw is available for use with a left hand insert.

The chuck is available for most brands of lathes.

THE CORONET CHUCK (Figs 118, 119, 120)

The Coronet chuck followed the 6-in-1 chuck and was probably the best-engineered product of its time. Its size was dictated by the machines available in the factory at the time. It has three sizes of expanding jaws 2⅞, 1¾ and 1in (73, 44 and 25mm) capacity. They work only in the expanding mode and are all operated by a centre boss.

The chuck can also be fitted with three sizes of collet jaws:

1in (25mm) collet with a capacity of ⅞-1in (22-25mm)
¾in (19mm) collet with a capacity of ⅝-¾in (16-19mm)
⅝in (16mm) collet with a capacity of ½-⅝in (13-16mm)

Coronet introduced the pin chuck with this chuck. The company calls it a centrifugal spigot which is an exact description of its action. They are machined with a right hand flat only to suit the Coronet lathes. There are four sizes 1⅜, 1, ¾, and ⅝in (35, 25, 19 and 16mm).

The small jaws are attached by springs to the centre boss which makes them extremely easy to assemble. I have had only one problem with the chuck; the jaws have very limited expansion, which demands accuracy in measuring and cutting the recesses.

118 Coronet expanding collet chuck – 1in (25mm) jaws fitted

*119 Coronet
collet chuck*

*120 Coronet
pin chuck*

121 Spannofix chucks

122 Spannofix chuck – moving the eccentric discs

THE SPANNOFIX CHUCKS (Figs 121, 122, 123)

These chucks are from the well known manufacturers, Luna in Sweden. There are two bodies, one for spigot holding and the other for bowl work where the chuck itself is inserted into a recess in the base of the bowl.

Each chuck is fitted with four eccentric discs, which can be offset and locked into the sides of a spigot or the sides of a recess cut in the bowl, enabling the work to be held firmly. Each disc has an annular radiused groove machined on the edge which provides positive gripping.

Two sizes are available – 3½ and 5in (88 and 128mm).

In bowl work a recess is cut to exactly the diameter of the chuck and in depth depending on the type of timber in use. A table gives details of sizing.

To assemble the bowl after turning the recess, first take the chuck and turn the discs so that they clear the periphery. Push the chuck into the recess and, using the special spanner, screw each disc in turn hard into the sides of the recess locking each with the nut.

Assembly of spigot work is carried out in a similar manner using the spigot body.

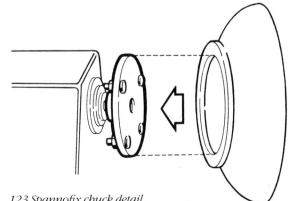

123 Spannofix chuck detail

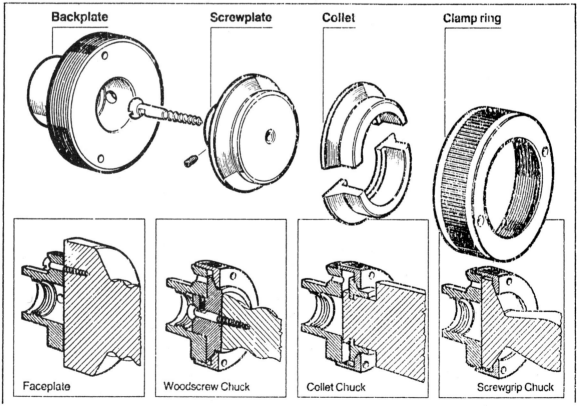

Backplate **Screwplate** **Collet** **Clamp ring**

Faceplate   Woodscrew Chuck   Collet Chuck   Screwgrip Chuck

MYFORD COMBINATION CHUCK (Fig 124)

This was the first of the combination chucks and was designed with the advice of Frank Pain by a company which has been a world leader in lathes for the home craftsman in wood. It has been designed for the right hand spindle of the Myford ML8 woodturning lathe. Its backplate or body can be used as a faceplate since it is drilled to receive three No 8 wood screws. A plate, which is located inside the body, receives a wood screw that is held securely in place with a socket setscrew. This plate is held in place by the outer ring and converts the chuck to a woodscrew chuck. A two-part collet converts the chuck into a collet chuck of 1½in (38mm) bore. The clamp ring and body together become a collar chuck; Fig 125 shows how the timber should be prepared for insertion in the collet chuck. The ⅜in (10mm) minimum gap shown is needed to permit the insertion of the collet and the use of the face spanner for locking the clamp ring. Place the clamp ring over the prepared end of the timber, insert the two halves of the collet, and screw the assembly on to the body; tighten with the spanner. Work of 2in (50mm) or less in diameter may be assembled using the body and ring only, preparation of timber for this mode is shown on page 41.

The chuck is very accurately made and the package includes body, screwplate with No 12 x 1¾in (45mm), wood screw, collet, clamp ring, face spanner, tommy bar, and Allen key. [NB] The latest collet has three segments.

ARNALL HEAVY DUTY COLLET CHUCK (Fig 126)

This is an extremely robust chuck designed to hold very large work, and also produced with limited aperture work in mind. It is a finely engineered job in mild steel with hardened steel jaws. Three sizes of collet are available – 25, 38 and 50mm (1, 1½, 2in) The chuck comprises body, collet, closing shroud, locking ring, 2 large C spanners, and sett gauge to suit the capacity of the collet. It is quite different in design from other collet chucks and is assembled by placing the collet into the internal thread in the body, placing the shroud over the body from the rear, up to the collet, and then screwing the locking ring over the body behind the shroud, finally engaging the left hand thread.

(top left) 124 Myford 4-in-1 chuck components

(left) 125 Myford 4-in-1 chuck – detail of the modes

126 Arnall collet chuck

127 Luna Autofix chuck

LUNA AUTOFIX CHUCK (Figs 127, 128)

Preparation of the timber must be done between centres since a spigot must be cut to the exact size of collet. A sett gauge is provided with the chuck for this purpose.

To assemble the work, locate the chuck on the spindle nose, unlock the locking ring, and slide the shroud back to free the jaws. Insert the workpiece into the collet and holding it in one hand, slide the shroud forward to engage the collet. Finally bring up the locking ring hand tight, check for concentricity, then use the spanners to lock hard. The chuck is so well engineered that it demands accurately fitting workpieces, as the amount of movement in the jaws is limited, but it is a fine job and well worth looking at if very large work is undertaken. There is no loss of centrality if the work has to be removed and re-placed.

The left-handed locking ring is so designed that if work should be interrupted and the turner forgets to tighten up the workpiece when the lathe is switched on, the ring will automatically run up and lock in place. The chuck is available to suit most lathes using an adaptor. (Can't stand the word shroud!)

This chuck is quite different from the others as it only fulfils one function – that of holding blocks for bowl and box work. There are three sizes of chuck needing holding recesses of 50, 75 and 100mm (2, 3, 4in). The chuck consists of the body, threaded to fit the Luna lathes, to which the functional part of the chuck is attached by means of an Allen screw. The chuck has a centre jaw, a segment of which slides into the cut recess in the workpiece when the assembly is turned by hand, firmly gripping it. A small lip around the periphery of the centre jaw bites into the edge of the recess to assist in holding.

The chuck has a novel feature – an adjustable cutting tool that assists in marking out the recess to ensure exact and close fitting of the chuck. It doesn't actually cut the recess; this must be done after the marking out. The recess is cut to the depth required for the particular size of chuck 3.5 to 6.5mm (1/8 to 1/4in). The tool is straightforward with no complications of design. It will serve as a great time saver and, if the user is equipped with saw tooth machine bits or Forstner bits of the correct size, the first stage of setting up and cutting the recess can be eliminated.

HARRISON COLLAR CHUCK (Fig 129)

129 Harrison collar chuck

A simple collar chuck, introduced with the Graduate lathe and suggested by the late Frank Pain, has had tremendous use in schools and colleges. Where the turner is constantly working in timber around 2in (50mm) diameter this will be found most useful. For preparation of the timber see page 41.

3-JAW CHUCK (Figs 130, 131)

These chucks are primarily for the metalturner, but many are in use and popular with the turner carrying out repetition work in a small workshop. The main objection to them is that the jaws tend to mark the timber, so finished or partly finished work cannot be held in them; the worker must always allow a waste end for holding. Many reject the chuck on grounds of safety, but if a good guard is fitted danger is reduced.

A development that will be welcomed by those turners with this type of chuck comes from Axminster Power Tools which has introduced sets of jaws designed with similar geometry to those of the preci-

130 Axminster add-on jaws for the engineer's chuck

sion combination chuck. These can be fitted to an existing chuck – or the turner can buy a chuck with fitted jaws which will grip in collet or expanding collet mode and are quite superb. The chuck is operated with a key in the normal way. Again, a safety guard is suggested.

4-JAW CHUCK (Fig 132)

The 4-jaw chuck is particularly useful where square sectioned work is to be held. Axminster can supply new chucks or modify existing ones to receive the new type jaws.

The standard of engineering is of the best and the company is able to fit new backplates to suit almost all the current woodturning lathes.

131 Axminster 3-jaw chuck with dovetail jaws

132 Axminster 4-jaw chuck with dovetail jaws

HOBBYMAT MULTI-PURPOSE CHUCK (Fig 133)

C.Z. Scientific Instruments have introduced a woodworking chuck for their Hobbymat variant lathe. The chuck is similar to the 4-jaw chuck of the metalworker. It has four reversible jaws which are self-centring, and they can be used to provide both compression and expansion clamping. They are not stepped like the metalworker's chuck, to offer variations of diameters within themselves. The chuck can be fitted with a fixed centre and a screw centre. The jaws can be removed permitting the chuck body to be used as a faceplate. A driving dog and suitable tools are also supplied.

(left) 133 Hobbymat multi-purpose chuck

DRILL CHUCK

This chuck is designed to hold boring tools in the tailstock of the lathe, but it can also be used in the headstock for holding small work. A ¾in (20mm) capacity chuck has the ¾ x 16in (20 x 400mm) screw of the Coronet lathe that enables it to be screwed directly to the headstock spindle. Screwed mandrels are available in Nos 1, 2 and 3 Morse tapers to permit its use elsewhere (Fig 134).

Other chucks are available fitted with the Morse taper of your lathe. Always buy a well known make since cheap chucks may have poorly fitting jaws – indeed, the jaws may not centre or close completely (Fig 135)

134 Drill chuck for Coronet lathe or for use with a screwed Morse taper mandrel

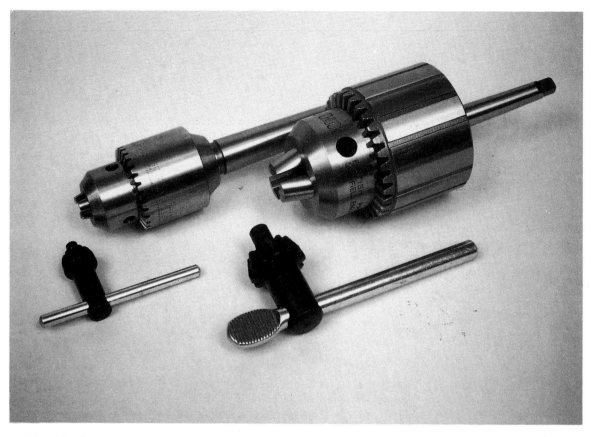

135 Drill chucks

*136 Pin chuck held
    in a drill chuck*

PIN CHUCK

The pin chuck is used by the instrument maker but when fitted into the drill or other type chuck it will be found useful for holding tiny pieces (Fig 136).

CHUCKS – GENERAL CARE IN USE

☐ Hold the finished work carefully when releasing it from the chuck.

☐ Protect all threaded parts against possible damage and occasionally wipe over with a lightly oiled cloth.

☐ Keep all component parts either in specially designed carrying cases or in a compartmented drawer or cupboard.

☐ Insert a pin chuck or an exact size round blank into the spigot/collet chuck when not in use to maintain its correct diameter.

☐ Keep all collets free from burrs otherwise they may mark the work badly. This applies equally to all components of the chuck.

☐ A chuck is the woodturner's friend – look after it and protect it from all ills.

6

TOOLRESTS AND OTHER EQUIPMENT

These are usually badly designed; often the work-manship leaves much to be desired, and more often than not they are not of the required length to suit a particular project. It is suggested that you make up a number using angle iron and mild steel rod of diameter to suit the lathe. Have them 50, 75, 100 and 150mm (2, 3, 4 and 6in) lengths or longer. Fit beech or similar even long-grained timber and shape them as shown. They are easy to maintain with a plane, and with variety in length they will meet most situations and can easily be replaced.

Position the toolrest slightly above centre when working between centres, slightly below for face-plate work, but if the tools are long and strong they will tend to be thicker than standard; in consequence, they will need to be a little lower. The important thing is that they must meet the timber with the cutting edge above centre. Scraping tools should meet the timber slightly *below* centre. When chiselling bring the toolrest up quite high so that cutting will take place at a point slightly below top dead centre.

137 Wooden toolrest

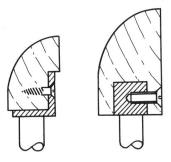

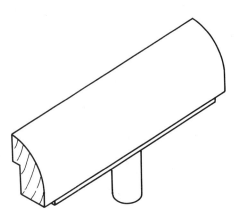

138 Detail of wooden toolrest

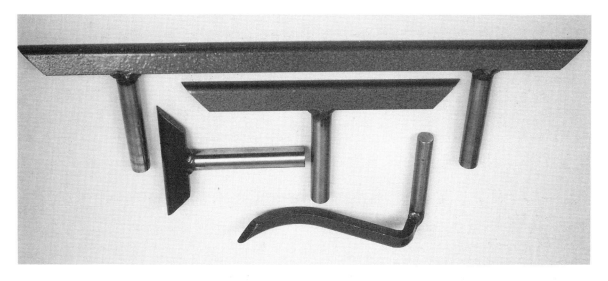

139 A selection of toolrests from Tyme Machines

Research into current methods has produced a number of rests particularly suitable for bowl work.

One such toolrest is suitable for normal shapes and sizes of bowls (Fig 140).

A useful addition to the short toolrest (for tiny bowl work), which is manufactured by Tyme Machines, is to drill a hole close to the left hand end of the rest into which a small checkpost can be inserted. This will be found particularly useful when using the gouge for inside bowl work. Turners will be aware of the fact that the gouge tends to move in the direction faced by the bevel, when placed on its side. The checkpost will stop this movement and also enable the cutting of very fine edges (Fig 141).

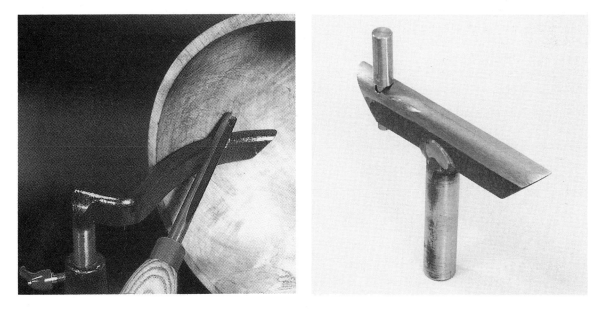

140 Short toolrest with check post

141 Toolrest for the smaller bowl

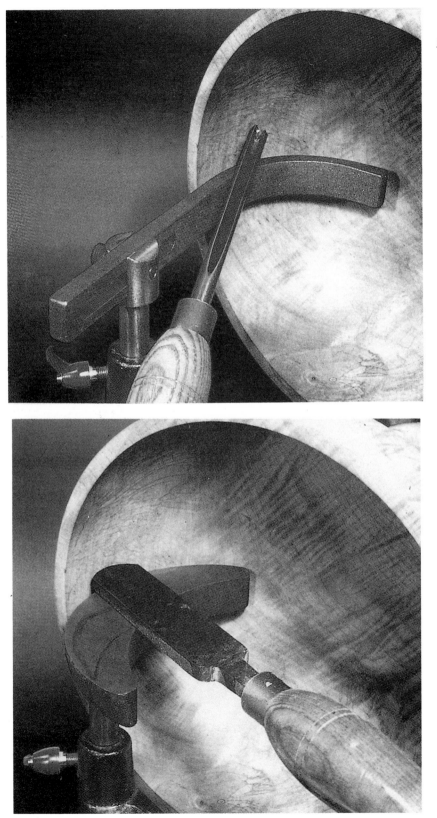

142 Adjustable rest for deep bowls

143 Cast iron rest for scraping tools

A completely different rest is the adjustable type, particularly suitable for large deep bowls. It is robust and ideal for the task (Fig 142).

Most of the early bowl rests were designed for scraping tools only – they could not be used with the gouge. One such rest is made in cast iron and has two positions for the round shaft so that it can be used in both left and right hand work positions (Fig 143).

THE BOWL TURNER'S MULTI-REST

The bowl turner's rest, from Treebridge (Figs 144, 145), marks a major step forward in toolrest design. It assists in the safe placement of tools, particularly gouges, when making bowls and similar work.

The photograph shows the rest, the top edge of which is flat nearest the point of work and drops sharply towards the user along its long side. The flat top is drilled to receive steel pins called checkposts. The rest, unlike those that have gone before, is designed to accommodate both cutting and scraping tools. The shape is an attempt to provide close support for the tool at the point of cut.

144 Bowl turner's Multi-rest

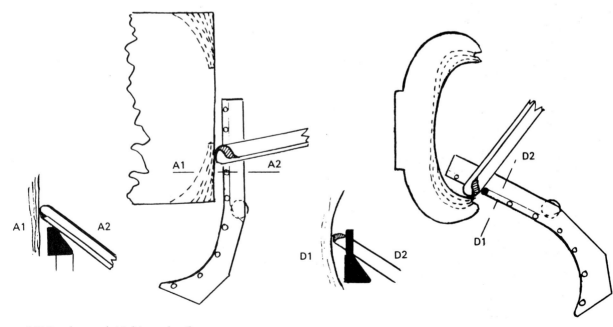

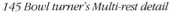
145 Bowl turner's Multi-rest detail

Gouges have a nasty habit, when placed on their side at the point of cutting, of moving, rapidly at times, in the direction in which the tool bevel is facing. When starting a bowl this usually means that the tool runs off the edge, where there is obviously no timber to support it, often with disastrous results. The multi-rest solves this since the checkpost can be placed at an exact position, the long edge of the tool comes against it, and the tool is under the complete control of the user.

Many turners are making articles which leave the natural edge on the rim. This creates a slight hazard since there are occasions where the gouge bevel is out of contact with the work surface for much of each revolution; the checkpost will be invaluable here and ensures that each and every cut can commence at the outside edge.

Whenever a fulcrum for the tool is needed this can be accurately placed.

Any part of the inside curved or straight edge of the rest can be used to support scrapers.

The shaped end can be inserted into deep work and the checkposts dropped in place to prevent the tool slipping off due to lack of sightline for the user.

For the beginner in particular, and indeed for most users, this toolrest must become a standard piece of equipment.

The user would be well advised to remove the paint from the top edges of the rest and polish the surfaces to ensure easy movement of the tool.

Solid bowl rest

A bowl rest made from solid round rod is the work of Barry Beck (Fig 146 Top).

ARNALL GATED TOOLREST (Fig 146 Bottom)

This is the only rest of its type in manufacture. It has been designed with limited aperture work in mind, to give safe and precise movement of scraping tools through a restricted entry hole.

The rest consists of a lower and upper bar, the latter prevents any downward or sideways tilt of the tool, which is particularly important with side cutting tools and with tools extended into a deep vessel.

146 (Top) Two-way bowl rest of solid rod
     (Bottom) Arnall gate toolrest

The rest is also fitted with a jack support which is adjustable to suit most lathes and serves to reduce vibration.

Several sizes of tool post are available, and they can be made to user specification.

Other equipment

With the high cost and shortage of good timber in mind and the desire to use some of the lesser known exotics, Bruce Boulter, a well known turner, devised a method of holding segmented or coopered timber safely on the lathe. The Boulter jig (Fig 147) is the result of his final experiments. It consists of a heavy faceplate which gives the chuck a fly wheel effect, eliminating much of the vibration set up in turning segmented stock. This heavy plate is slotted to receive three different sizes of clamping arms, which in turn secure the workpiece; a Jubilee clip placed around the assembly holds the clamping arms in place. A wooden disc on the faceplate centralises the blank. It is then possible to turn the inside of the work accurately to a finished state.

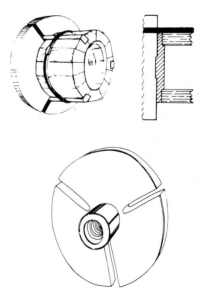

147 Boulter jig

Sizing tool

This was popular more than 100 years ago. The sizing tool has been re-designed by Craft Supplies (Fig 148) and most ¼in (6mm) parting tools will fit into it, although it is recommended for use with the ⅜in (10mm) Sorby beading and parting tool and the ⅜in (10mm) Bedan tool which is ground on one side only. It is an ideal tool for accurate sizing, eliminating the need for calipers.

In use, rest the rear of the C against the back of the work and carefully lower it to bring the parting tool into action.

enclosed-form shapes and the other for deep narrow forms such as vases and barrels. The normal shape of caliper cannot be used for most narrow entry work but these make the task simple. The actual wall thickness can be measured and read off against a datum line on the face of the calipers. Three sizes are available – 330, 220 and 125mm (13, 8¾, and 5in) (Fig 149).

A sett gauge is provided with the Arnall collet chuck that can be used to check the stub which must be turned at one end of the workpiece in order to insert it into the chuck (Fig 150).

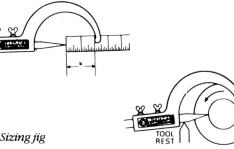

148 Sizing jig

TOOL REST

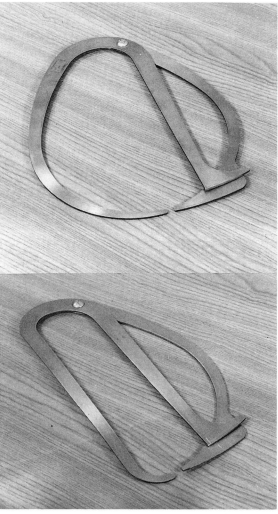

ARNALL GAUGES

Complementary to the chuck, and tools for limited aperture turning designed by the Arnalls in Australia, are two pairs of calipers. These are wall-thickness registering calipers in a set of two, one for wide

149 Arnall wall thickness registering calipers

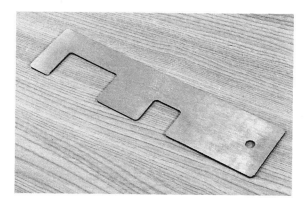

150 Arnall sett gauge

151 Adjustable calipers, dividers and trammel

CALIPERS AND MARKING OUT EQUIPMENT

The most important of these is the double ended caliper (Fig 151). It enables a constant watch to be kept on wall thickness. This caliper transfers the measurement from one end to the other, giving an instant visual reference. Preferably buy a plated one and keep it close to the lathe.

DIVIDERS

These are useful for setting out, and can also be employed to check tiny measurements. They are best sprung, and again a 6in (150mm) size would be suitable.

Where measurement is critical and there is a chance of movement of the arms, it is best to use the sprung type calipers. An outside 6in (150mm) size would meet most needs.

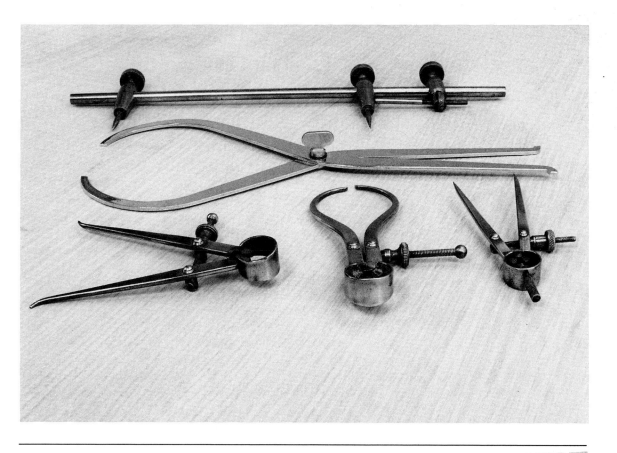

*152 Woodturning
mandrels*

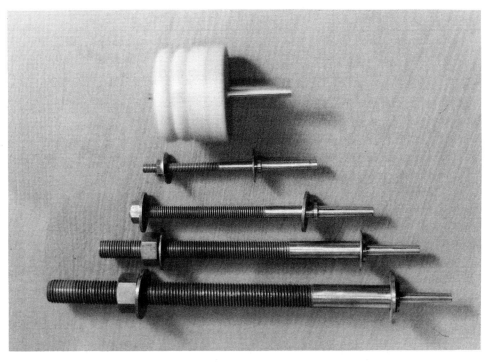

WOODTURNING MANDRELS (Fig 152)

I used to turn wheels using an assembly with two end blocks and a length of dowel. That was easy, and the blocks could be used endlessly. But mandrels simplify the job even more; they are made from precision ground carbon steel. Each mandrel is ground No 1 Morse taper at one end and is drilled at the opposite end to receive the running centre. The straight portion of the mandrel is threaded and nuts and washers complete it.

They are available in: ¼ x 3in (6 x 75mm)

3⁄8 x 4½in (10 x 115mm)

½ x 7½in (12 x 190mm)

¾ x 11in (20 x 280mm)

1 x 15in (25 x 380mm)

Pre-bored stock can be assembled and safely turned between centres.

The flexible drive can be used with the electric drill or with any small machine to which it can be coupled. Fitted with abrasive pads, flap wheels, and other abrasive heads, it has become very popular with many professional and home turners.

Often we have problems in removing screwed-on components from the headstock mandrel. Every lathe needs a leather washer placed between the face of the spindle and the back of the chuck. This will help to avoid jamming. However should the problem arise, there are several solutions. I have mentioned elsewhere that I use a plumber's chain wrench for this; it is quite a light tool and has never failed, but the teeth can bite into the chuck or faceplate and precautions should be taken to avoid this (Fig 153). Another solution is the Zyliss Strongboy

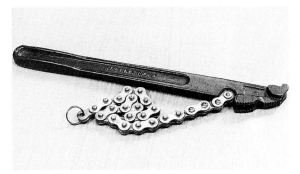

153 Chain wrench

154 Zyliss Strongboy used to remove a cone

which is simply a flexible steel strap that can be sized to suit the job. It is not as strong as the wrench but ideal for the smaller components (Fig 154).

A flexible template is essential for the woodturner – I use one with steel needles which can be pushed into place to copy any shape. I often have two clipped together for use on longer work (Fig 155).

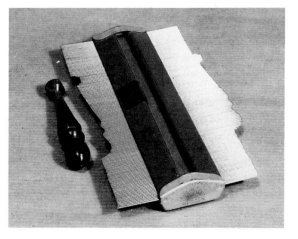

155 Template with adjusting steel needles

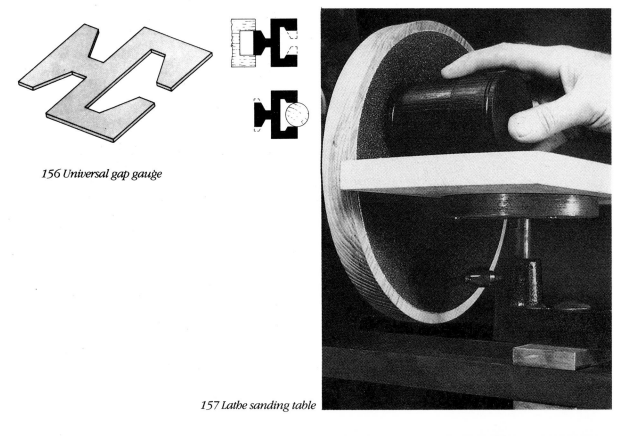

156 Universal gap gauge

157 Lathe sanding table

158 Ducat lathe steady

Another addition is the brass-sheet gap gauge (Fig 156). These can be made to suit the turner and are particularly useful for repetition turning where accuracy is vital. They are available for internal and external diameters ranging from ½ to 2in (12 to 50mm), in ¹⁄₁₆in (1.5mm) thick material that can be filed easily and quickly to the size needed.

A lathe sanding table may be found useful for trimming the undersides of bowls and other turnings (Fig 157). I am not very happy about having these permanently attached. They can be slightly dangerous at the outboard end of the lathe when turning is taking place inboard. The one shown consists of a mounting flange which can be dropped into the toolrest holder. It can be fitted with a table of convenient size made from an accurately planed piece of beech or similar even-grained hardwood. The disc is made from a piece of good quality hardwood or plywood which can either be attached to a little-used faceplate and left permanently in place, or alternatively, a faceplate ring can be fitted to suit the size of jaws you use in the precision combination chuck.

The flanges are available in stem sizes to suit different hand-/tool-rest supports:

⅝in (16mm)
¾in (19mm)
1in (25mm)
20mm (¾in)
25mm (1in)
30mm (1³⁄₁₆in)
35mm (1⅜in)

Lathe steadies are not commonly used, but when the turning of long thin work is undertaken, it is almost impossible to do without one. I made my first after much experiment many years ago for my Myford lathe, and it works well (see page 145).

A production job which is probably the ultimate solution is the Ducat (Fig 158). It consists of a twin roller assembly that is controlled by a form of friction ratchet and is under constant locking pressure from a spring which also pushes the roller assembly forward. The two rollers are 18mm (¹¹⁄₁₆in) in diameter, and they will support work from 5mm (³⁄₁₆in) up to 60mm (2⅜in) in diameter. Three different stem sizes are available to suit the lathe toolrest holder ⅝in, ¾in (16mm and 19mm) and also 1in (25mm).

7

TOOLS FOR CUTTING

Significant changes have taken place in recent years in the methods of production, and in the design and the material used for woodturning tools. These tools tended to be of traditional shape and size and were made of carbon steel, forged under spring hammers and ground by hand. They were adequate, fulfilled their allotted task, and generally satisfied the worker craftsmen. The greater demand for tools all over the world and the wider circle of users, both professional and amateur, demanded a closer look.

A partial failure to understand fully the function of these tools resulted in the production of poorly formed gouges ground to unbelievably bad bevels. Marples, under the Record Ridgway umbrella, produced the first redesigned gouge in the ¼in (6mm) spindle size. This was made from round stock, the flute milled and ground with its end an exact shape of the little finger end. A redesigned parting tool, stamped out and taper ground throughout its length, provided relief from the heat of friction in parting off. These tools were made without forging and eliminated human errors in production.

Peter Child and his son, Roy, through their teaching experience, were quick to assess the need and

159 Henry Taylor Superflute gouge

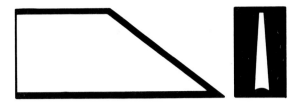

160 Fluted parting tool

offer solutions. Unfortunately they did not have a manufacturing facility, but they did bring about a number of far-reaching changes.

The Superflute gouge for bowl turning (Fig 159) employing high speed steel for the first time, arrived at the best shaping of the flute, eliminated all forging, used round section material, and gave a strong tool with immense power. Roy also took the parting tool and completely changed its look and action. Using high speed steel, he cut a flute on the underside, along the total length of the blade, and gave it a bevel on the top only. Tapered on both sides to give a trapezium section, it not only cut down the friction, but the fluting formed two curved cutting points which produced a slicing cutting action. This has proved to be the best parting tool ever, and although it tends to mark the T rest it certainly cuts without tearing end grain (Fig 160).

The use of scraping chisels has long been a subject of controversy and many abhor their use. Several changes have taken place – stricter attention to the ground angle, heavier section material, longer and stronger handles, and high-speed-steel-tipped tools. The universal tool with detachable tips has also arrived.

The traditional bowl gouge was long and strong, deep-fluted and ground square across at its business end. No one had ever questioned the need for the square across grinding, and manufacturers had not bothered since the 'square across' form was simple to produce. Gerry Glaser in the United States had noticed that Bob Stockdale, of world-renowned bowl-turning fame, used a gouge with a round nose and a flute form similar to the spindle gouge. This he copied in round HSS and produced a superbly strong and extremely efficient bowl and spindle gouge in one.

The world's biggest, and arguably the best, range of cutting tools comes under the brand name of Robert Sorby Ltd, as distinct from Robert Sorby and Sons Ltd. This new company has changed the face of the woodturning tools industry having not only studied the problems of the turner in depth but also critically examining the materials and methods of production used. They have listened to many craftsmen, users, and employed executives, who know the business and have put together the ingredients of success.

Robert Sorby Ltd lists upwards of 60 different tools, many of them innovative and solving some of the problems that have afflicted the learners in the past. These tools look good in every respect from the elegant purpose designed Bocote handles of the de luxe range to the hand polished handles in ash, holding blades of top quality high speed steel, designed for purpose, and superbly machined.

Every gouge is milled and ground to correct shape and depth from round steel, with bowl gouges of great strength, well up to the task of heavy cutting to any depth, even in the most difficult timbers. Gone are the problems inherent in the forged tools, especially spindle gouges which were so often too shallow and are now perfectly shaped to make coving and similar work a pleasure. The old flat roughing gouge has been replaced by a deep section tool ground across the face. This can be used, not only for roughing down stock, but also on its side as a roughing chisel.

There is also a range of parting tools. The diamond section with parallel sides so popular in North America, is still made, but there are also several sizes of straight tools: the fluted, fully relieved style, designed by Child and the Bedan, a tool ground on one side only and much favoured on the continent. The parting tool is not yet perfect, but at least we have a choice in HSS, which lessens the burning inherent in the carbon steel variety.

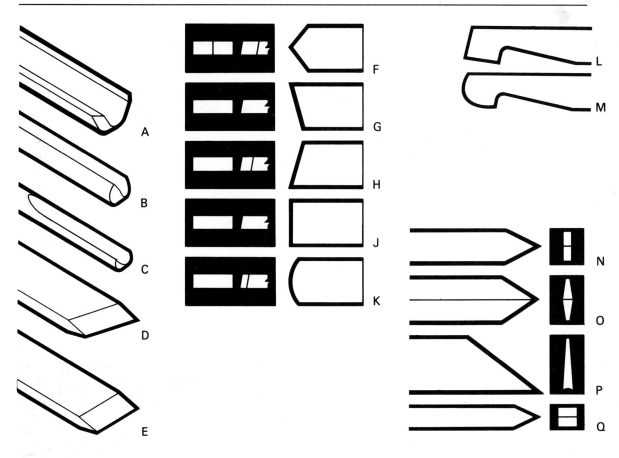

CUTTING TOOL SHAPES AND SECTIONS

161 Cutting tool shapes and sections

A	Roughing out gouge
B	Bowl gouge
C	Spindle gouge
D	Skew chisel
E	Square across chisel
F	Diamond point scraper
G	Left hand skew scraper
H	Right hand skew scraper
J	Square end scraper
K	Round nose scraper
L and M	Side cutting scrapers
N	Standard parting tool
O	Diamond section parting tool
P	Fluted parting tool
Q	Beading and parting tool

SORBY SKEW CHISEL (Figs 162, 163)

The skew chisel is the plane of the woodturner – he must master its use or join the ranks of the defeated and take up the scraper. To hear some people (who ought to know better) one would think that it must be the most difficult cutting tool ever devised, and one could almost assume from this that sales must be so low that manufacturing such a tool might be considered uneconomic and their disappearance imminent. Not so: sales are better than ever.

To examine critically the skew we need to look back a little at the early ones. Chisels were made both skew and square across; some had two bevels, one each side, and others were ground on one side only. The latter style meant that the user needed a right and a left handed tool in skew form. The latter I understand were favoured by the patternmaker; I saw one such worker in an engineering company turning a six foot across pattern using a two inch chisel ground on one side only with the long corner removed. A fantastic sight, but I had no ambition to climb into his pit and have a go myself. All the bevels (Cannels in Sheffield) were rolled; that is they were round, not flat. I am sure that this practice must have given rise to problems in cutting since sharpening produced a very short bevel, and the included angle between the bevel faces was upwards of 90°. Thus in order to get the chisel to cut the turner had to raise his handle very high and, as only a small bevel rested on the wood, there was a great tendency for the chisel to be pushed towards the user resulting in the much talked-of dig-in. Even if the user recognised the fault it would still be quite difficult for him to correct without the use of adequate grinding facilities. In 1964 Marples changed to flat grinding and stopped the manufacture of the single bevel chisel. Other makers followed suit, and one would have thought that there would be an immediate improvement of the chisel in use. Unfortunately many

162 Sorby oval skew

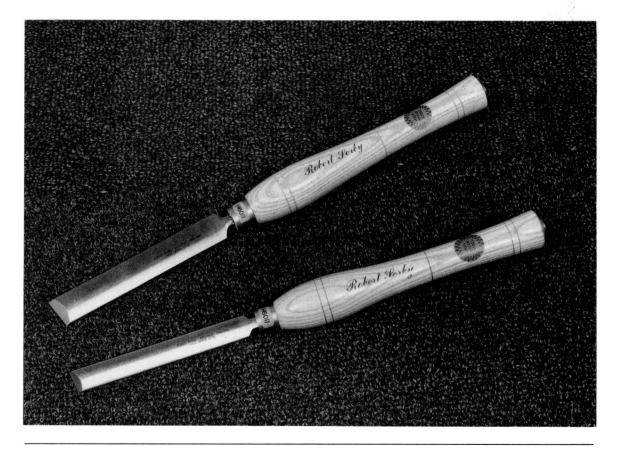

craft advisers and school folk tended to describe the cutting tools as too dangerous for boys. Few seemed to understand the technique needed to use the chisel in safety and comfort. This tool is the plane of the lathe and it should produce similar results; its application to the work should also be similar. The first rule of the plane in use is to sharpen the cutter to produce a hairline of cutting edge. The cap iron is then attached and set to break the shaving and roll it out of the escapement of the plane body. The cutting unit, when set up in the plane, reveals this black hairline of cutting edge just showing across the mouth of the plane when looking across the sole. With the lever cap in place planing can commence – the cutter cuts and lifts the shaving, the cap iron breaks it just ahead of the cutter, and away it goes. The timber sings (just like any good Welshman) and then it shines, having been burnished by the polished sole of the plane after the point of cut. The action of the skew is exactly the same as that of the plane – the edge does the cutting when the tool handle is lifted, and the bevel following behind polishes the timber. The oft-quoted advice to 'let the bevel rub', has if followed a two-fold benefit – the support of the tool during its travel across the timber and the polishing. The bevel therefore is the sole, and it must be finished as perfectly as the plane sole. One problem

that arises when the bevel of the chisel rests on the timber is that, when the handle is raised, the chisel rests on the tool- and hand-rest with the corner of its long edge in contact. The long edges of the chisel usually have a fine finish, indeed they are almost sharp cutting edges, which cut into the rest, leaving small grooves. These arrest the progress of the chisel along the work. Invariably we radius the corners to remove this sharpness; I polish mine on the rubberised abrasive wheel to produce a better sliding action. I can rest the chisel firmly on the work and it will slide smoothly along.

The manufacturer has paid too little attention to the chisel – often, as I have said repeatedly, the user has been ignored. But, dear reader, be not dismayed; don't sell your lathe and take up knitting or beating the wife. Sorby has produced a chisel that will help to relieve the difficulties, making chiselling easy and instilling great confidence, particularly in the beginner.

The line drawing (Fig 163) shows a section of the material used for the oval skew chisel. This U section is revolutionary in its rolling action and will obviously be a little more expensive than the traditional material, but the benefits are considerable. The chisel now rests on a purposed designed curved face which gives a decidedly better contact with the rest.

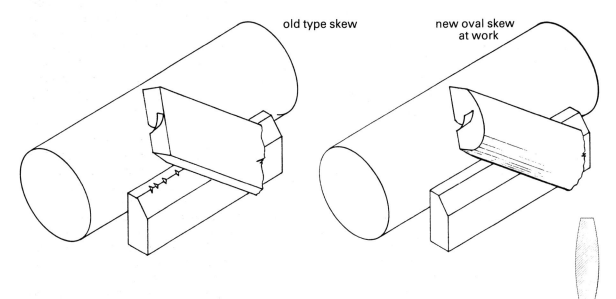

163 Cross section of the material and action of the skew

The linishing on this blade is the best I have ever seen, serves to assist the sliding of the tool along the rest. The section also makes the cutting of curves considerably easier, there is no corner now to hazard the radiusing movement of the chisel; thus beading and curving generally are less difficult than formerly. This is particularly noticeable if one uses the centre of the cutting edge for beads as I do. In addition, the chisel can be used on its flat edge to employ the long corner for squaring timber and for stepping. The chisel is fitted with the handle now standard on Sorby turning tools. This handle, which is of French polished ash, permits light but firm holding, which in turn encourages the featherweight cut needed for perfect finishing.

Sorby has four scraping chisels in HSS, a set of heavy scrapers in carbon steel and also scrapers tipped in high speed steel. To complete the range there is a universal scraper which has three interchangeable cutters, each with four cutting edges (Fig 164).

164 Universal scraper with three cutters

The original shapes of the heavy scrapers were those introduced by the late Peter Child. The latest are made from HSS, 1½in by ⅜in (38mm by 10mm) material and seek to meet every scraping requirement. Left and right hand skew spades can be used for squaring the sides of boxes and similar work, while the forward edge eases the work of flatting the bottoms. The included angle between the two cutting faces is about 80°, making it impossible for both edges to cut at the same time – an excellent cutting

feature. A side scraper eases the problem of undercutting inside a bowl, and a full round edge copes with most other situations.

Two sizes of ring tool have been introduced and although these differ in some respects from the Scandinavian variety the cutting action is the same.

The miniaturist has not been forgotten, with a set of five tools that are exact replicas of their big brothers with handles in both ash and bocote (Fig 165).

Handles have long been a problem – they are so much an individual thing. Sorby produced handles which are shaped to fit the hand comfortably to relate in some measure to the size of the tool blade and the type of cutting for which it is designed.

Handle sizes are:

	Ferrule Size	Length
micro	⁹⁄₁₆in (15mm)	6¼in (170mm)
small	¾in (20mm)	8½in (215mm)
standard	¾in (20mm)	10in (255mm)
	⅞in (22mm)	10in (255mm)
long and	1in (25mm)	11¾in (300mm)
strong	1¼in (32mm)	11¾in (300mm)
extra strong	1in (25mm)	17in (430mm)
	1¼in (32mm)	17in (430mm)

A range that would seem to cover adequately any collection of tools.

The Luna Company of Sweden has a range of tools for woodturning. Apart from the chisels and shallow gouges which are similar to those of the UK, the parting tool is of parallel section and ground on one side only. Scraping chisels are also available for inside working with some specified for right hand working.

An unusual chisel called the Luna Speedy (Fig 166) is really a scraping tool fitted with a circular cutter which can be turned round so that all the edge can be used; it can be reversed and replacements are available. The blades are ground at an angle of 38° in two sizes 14 and 18mm (⁹⁄₁₆in and (¹¹⁄₁₆in). The tool, with wooden handle, is 400mm (16in) long.

The Speedcut is quite different from any other, consisting of a tubular metal handle, covered in plastic, to which is fitted a clamping device that will accept a range of differently shaped cutters. The handle revolves so that the scraping cutter always lies flat on the toolrest. The knives can be adjusted to different cutting depths against a chip thickness limiter and locked by means of a screw. Cutter

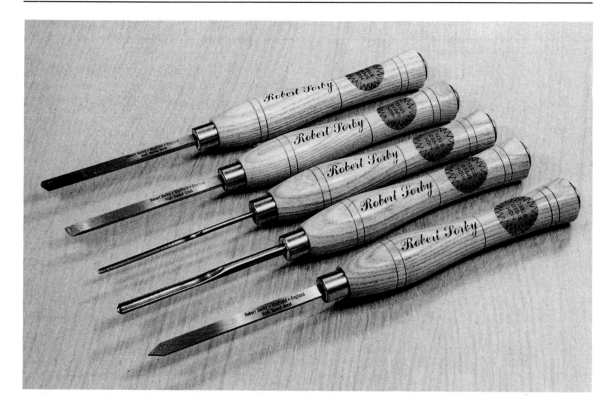

165 Sorby micro tools

166 Luna speedy

shapes are round nose, half round right, half round left, vee shape and parting, with blanks also available.

Bowl gouges are not shown since the tools for bowl work 'according to the cutting method' are called 'Slow motion' and described as special 'turning eyes' intended for internal use (Fig 167). They are available in sizes 16 and 25mm (⅝ and 1in), 400mm (16in) long (see page 126 for more detail of the ring tool).

Another tool having a similar cutting action to the ring is the Slow Motion II which is a hook intended for internal use according to the 'cutting method' (Fig 168). Again it is available in 16 and 25mm (⅝ and 1in) size rings and 400mm (16in) in length (see page 126 for more detail on the hook tool).

Teknatool of New Zealand which produces a traditional range also has a number of unique bowl turning tools. The Hi-turn tools have screw-on tips of high quality HS steel. These are fastened to heavy solid steel shafts. Packages of tips are available in three different forms. The ¾in (19mm) bowl and roughing gouge (Fig 169) is for heavy work, but the

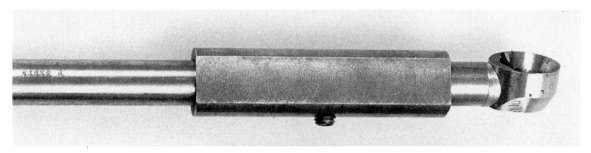

167 Luna turning eye or ring

168 Luna hook or Slow Motion II

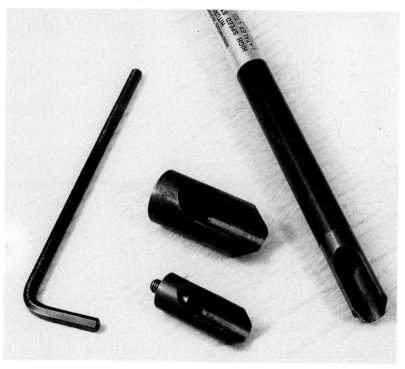

169 Teknatool Hi-turn

user could have a number of tips ground to cover various options. I would have one ground across for roughing, one at 40° for general bowl work, with another at 65° for deep bowl use.

The ½in (13mm) bowl gouge may well be more popular with some users, but I would still recommend several tips, as with the heavier gouge.

Another unique tool is the ½in (13mm) hollowing tool (Fig 170). This one has a circular tip and has been designed to hollow out the insides of vases and goblets where space is restricted. Its action is not dissimilar from that of the ring tool, but the shavings cannot pass through the ring because they have to be deflected, as in the gouge. The circular tips are held in place with a cap and screw.

The tip can be turned to give extra life. It is set at an angle and extra ones are listed. A special technique for sharpening ring and hook tools is detailed on page 166.

These tools could provide the answer for turners who sharpen by the grinding method, and they are cheaper than the solid HSS variety. They certainly perform like the normal tool, and although many traditionalists will shudder, I am sure they are here to stay.

170 Teknatool hollowing tool

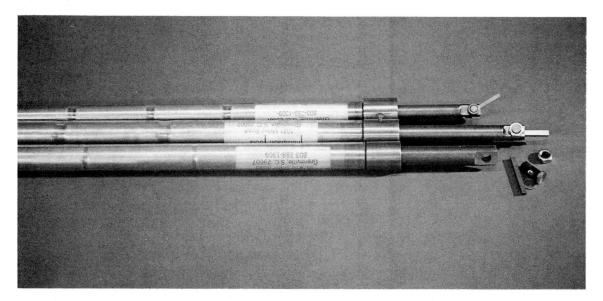

171 Jim Thompson turning tools

Another departure from the traditional is seen in the range of tools from Jim Thompson in the USA (Fig 171). He has not only designed a 'varispeed' lathe with a difference (see page 175), but the tools to go with it. The tools consist of a number of shaped cutting bits in HSS which actually substitute for the centre portion of the gouge. These are held in a slot at the end of a solid bar and can be placed at any angle. The rod in turn slides in a hollow steel handle and can be adjusted to any length. This extension of length provides greater leverage and easier control. The bits can cut on the shear, or can be used in the scraping mode. Jim Thompson uses these tools constantly.

They are made in:

length	length extended	weight	bit size
¾ x 30in (20 x 760mm)	50in (1,270mm)	6lb	³/₁₆in (5mm)
⅞ x 34in (22 x 865mm)	60in (1,525mm)	9lb	³/₁₆ and ¼in (5 and 6mm)
1 x 36in (25 x 915mm)	64in (1,625mm)	12lb	³/₁₆ and ¼ (5 and 6mm)

A departure in materials is seen in the cobalt alloy tipped tools from the Cherry Wood and Tools Company in the USA. The company has also made some changes in traditional design. Cobalt alloy is temperature stable, needing no initial heat treatment, and it cannot be annealed by the heat built up during fast moving turning. The extended life of the cutting edge is extraordinary. Another advantage is that annealing during grinding is much less likely than with ordinary carbon tool steels.

In the range are a 1³/₈in (35mm), a ¾in (20mm) roughing gouge and a ½in (13mm) shallow gouge. The skew chisel is 1¼in (32mm) and its heel has been slightly rounded over – it is suggested that this will facilitate control when making rolling cuts. The company as yet has not produced a deep bowl gouge.

The ¼in (6mm) parting tool is parrot-nose shape and can also be used as a boring tool in both spindle and faceplate work. It works well but takes a little getting used to since it has to be pushed forward into the work – unlike the normal parting tool which cuts when the handle is raised with the bevel resting on the work.

The more normal-shaped parting tool, with parallel sides, has a long grinding bevel on the top side.

Tungsten carbide tipped tools are common in the field of routing where materials vary from softwood through hardwood to manmade materials, all of which take their toll on any but the best edges. The high speeds at which a router operates cannot be compared with the slower speeds of the turner and the choice of TCT would perhaps not be favoured by him, having in mind the need for a green wheel or diamond wheel for sharpening – an expensive item to add to the kit. At the same time these tips can be very accident-prone – one tool striking another can shatter a fine edge. Nevertheless Tools, Etc of Louisville in Kentucky have introduced a range of tipped tools based on traditional lines; both shallow gouges and skew chisels. There is a new design in parting tools; this one has a round nose, and it works well though it does tend to throw up a little around the edges of the cut. These tools perform so well that it is difficult to quarrel with the makers, one must indeed congratulate them on their initiative and regret that they have not as yet, produced a bowl gouge.

Gouges very similar to the Superflute of UK manufacture come from R. Jackson of Oak Ridge, New Jersey. These are called J gouges and there are two sizes ¾in (20mm) and ⁹/₁₆in (13mm), 25 and 31in (625 and 785mm) in length. The tools are coated to increase the hardness at the cutting edge to Rockwell 70, giving a longer lasting edge and a resistance to rust.

A company in Australia has introduced a range of tools in M2 HS steel, handled in indigenous hardwoods fitted with ferrules machined from heavy brass tubing. Boral Cyclone has been making precision tools in HSS for the past 25 years and is well versed in the requirements of cutting tools. The tools are of good weight and are well balanced. A full range of roughing, spindle and bowl gouges are listed together with five sizes of skew chisel. The parting tool is straight sided and there is also a range of scraping tools.

Jerry Glaser in California is a first-class engineer as well as a woodturner who has studied cutting tools both in regard to materials and design. He has discussed the problems with some of the world's leading woodturners and had them confirm his findings. Years back he produced a gouge (Fig 172) based on the one used by Bob Stocksdale, the well

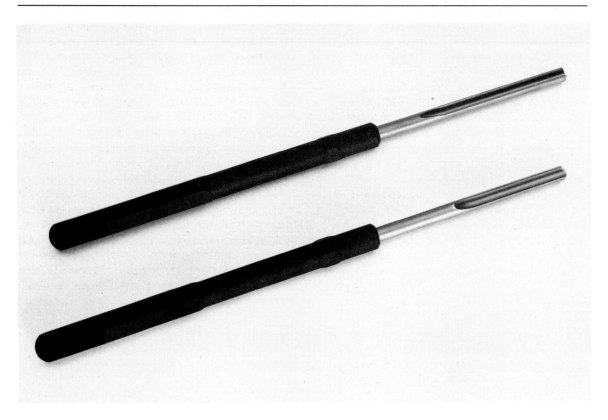

172 Glaser bowl gouge with metal handle

known Californian turner, but his was in M-4 high speed steel having a 4% vanadium content. This I have used ever since and it cannot be faulted, but Jerry is ever ready to experiment and he now has a complete range of turning tools in A-11 tool steel. This contains 10% vanadium and 2% carbon for highest wear resistance and easily out-performs all high-speed steel tools (Jerry's quote).

ALLOY STEEL

Jerry Glaser was kind enough to supply the following detail on tool steels suitable for turning tools.

T-1 is the type of HSS in fairly common use in turning tools

M-2 is the HSS used in many cutting tools including turning tools on both sides of the Atlantic

M-4 is an improved HSS with 4% vanadium used in the earlier Stocksdale and other tools by Glaser

A-11 is now used for all Glaser turning tools and has proved superior to all the others in present use, having been tested by many of the leading turners of today.

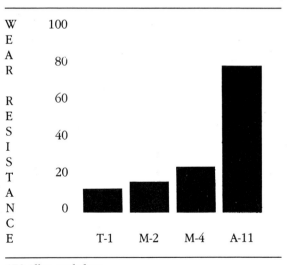

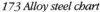

173 Alloy steel chart

The material is produced by an advanced metallurgy process to result in fine and uniformly distributed wear resistant vanadium carbides (see chart Fig 173). The tools are hardened and triple-tempered in a vacuum furnace for optimum combination of hardness and toughness. Small and uniform carbides make the tools far easier to grind and hone, and I can certainly confirm this in the tools I have used.

The argument about tool weight has been going on for a long time and, in the main, weight has tended to be added by increasing the size of the handles. This reached a ridiculous state, where handles were just too big for the average man to hold, one needed a shovel-like hand. A number of turners of my acquaintance have bored out the ends of the wood handles and weighted them with lead. Jerry has considered this and produced a handle in 1⅛in (30mm) aluminium alloy of hexagonal section. It is heat treated for strength, shot peened for non-slip grip, and finished in a hard anodised black.

I'm not enthusiastic about metal handles, preferring the warm welcoming feel of wood, but this tool handles well under tough conditions. It doesn't run off the bench either. Jerry's gouges are in deep and shallow section, and I applaud the rounding of the long edges of chisels to ease the passage along the toolrest and around the curves.

From this turner explorer we can also look forward to the development of the boring bar, particularly for use in deep limited aperture work.

Rude Osolnik, one of the famed woodturners of the USA, is self taught and has not only devised his own tools (Fig 174) but has altered some traditional tools to suit his work. He has proved the worth of high speed steel tools over very many years. An English manufacturer has now produced these tools in M-2 HSS hardened to a Rockwell of 62-64. Rude uses a chisel with a round and ground well-back

174 The tools of Rude Osolnik

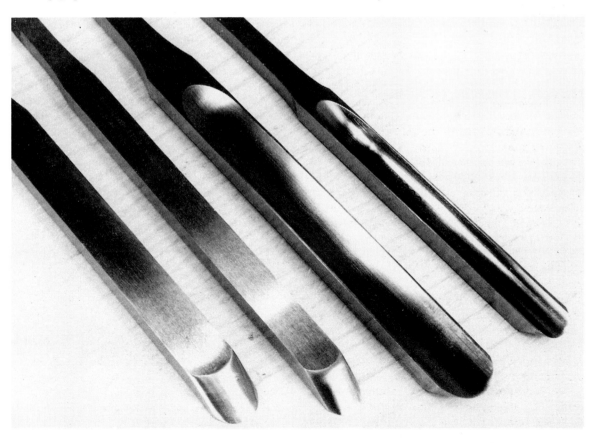

*175 Stewart tools – the arm
    brace and padded handle
    fitted with the hooker*

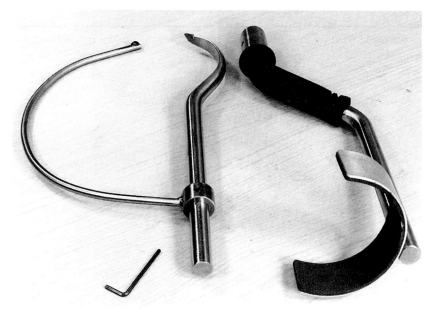

cutting-edge on almost everything he turns. I saw this type of tool used in the UK only by a patternmaker many years ago. I made a copy and used it between centres but never inside a bowl. In recent years I had one made by Sorby in HSS and have used it with great success on shallow bowls and also between centres. Rude's blades differ in over-all shape from all the others. The set comprises ½ and ⅝in (12 and 15mm) round nose chisels, ⅝in (15mm) square ended chisel and ½, ⅝ and ¾in (12, 15 and 20mm) gouges – all of which are fairly shallow. They are beautifully made and supplied unhandled.

Dennis Stewart, to whom I refer in a cameo on page 182, is probably the greatest innovator of his time; not only in his work but in the tools which he has devised to meet situations which cannot be solved with traditional tools.

Each tool is not only extremely efficient and versatile in its own right, but it can be used as a component in a system to increase dramatically its versatility. By making the components interchangeable, many tools can be created from a basic set. Each cutting component is replaceable, thus the main items will last a lifetime. There are two types of handle quite unlike any handle ever made (Fig 175). The one has an arm brace designed for control,

safety, and comfort when reaching extreme distances over the toolrest. This arm brace at the end of the handle provides a substantial amount of leverage control, yet still allows the arm to be in a comfortable working position. The padded hand grip, being offset from the toolshank, provides excellent rotational control. At the same time operational stresses on the hand and arm that occur when using a horizontal handle are relieved. The firm neoprene grip will absorb vibration and the handle has a socket which allows for quick changes of component.

The pistol handle provides the same comfort and

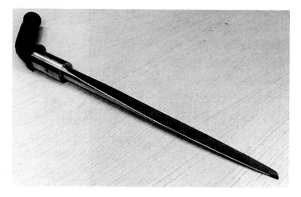

176 Pistol handle fitted to the slicer

control but is for closer application for very precise cutting (Fig 176). A new tool, the slicer, is used to make deep plunge cuts at any angle, removing whole pieces of wood at a time. The slicer can also be used as a wood saver, allowing the turner to remove from the inside of a block a cone which can be used to make several more bowls. The slicer also can be used to cut tapered rings which can be stack-laminated in turn to make bowls and other forms. The tool can also be used for parting. It is made from a steel alloy for rigid strength and toughness, with a carbide tip.

An 'omnitool' is multi-functional with inter-changeable tips (Figs 177, 178). The shaker tip has a left point on one end and a right point on the other which is used for spindle work and for shaping various sorts of bowls and vessels. It is very good for thin walled items. There is also a side cutting tip, which

177 Omnitool with replaceable tip

178 Tips for the omnitool, the chattertool and the scraper

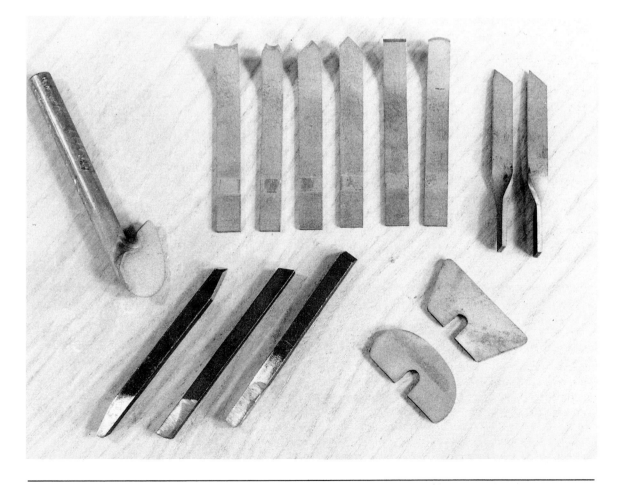

has a square nose with a round nose on the other end. This tip also works well on end grain for quick removal of material. Using a set of chatter blades decorative textures can be added. The omnitool can also be used for boring, by inserting a drill bit; it is probably the most versatile tool ever made for woodturning.

A super scraper is designed for making very smooth finishing cuts, both on the inside and outside of a bowl. It has a four-position blade attachment system and two replaceable blades, making eight separate tools.

A hooker makes limited aperture turning much easier and safer. The carbide tip has a long life. A special hook design allows for very aggressive cuts, without rotational force on the tool. It also permits access where the traditional tool could not be used (Fig 179).

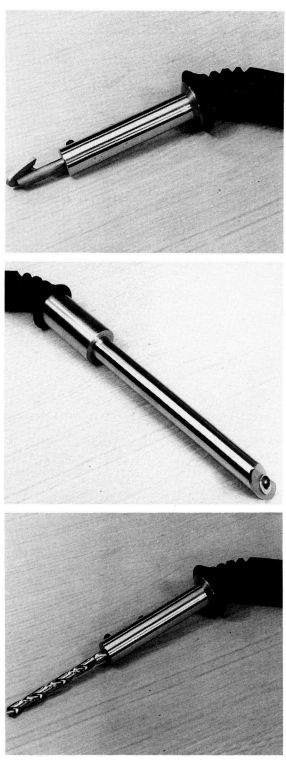

179 The hooker for limited aperture work

A wall thickness gauge can be attached to the hooker to make it easy to judge the thickness while turning. It can also be attached to other tools in the set.

The tools are available as a complete set (Figs 180, 181, 182) comprising arm brace and pistol handle, slicer, super scraper, hooker, wall gauge, omnitool, omni accessory set, chatter blade and sil-carbide wheel.

(left) 180 The super scraper

(centre left) 181 Handle with scraper blade fitted

(lower left) 182 Handle with boring bit fitted

(below) 183 The chisels of Richard Raffan

A basic set comprises the arm brace and pistol handles, slicer, super scraper, omnitool and grinding wheel.

The chatter set includes the deluxe chatter tool and chatter blades.

The deep and hollow set includes arm brace handle, wall gauge, hooker, slicer and wheel.

Richard Raffan is well known for his woodturning and for his variations on the traditional chisel (Fig 183). His skew chisel has a radiused edge which assists in general planing between centres and also makes for much safer bead cutting. He also has a range of scraping chisels that have a curved edge, making it possible to 'fine face' the insides of bowls and similar work.

The blades are between 10 and 12in (255 and 305mm) in length, but they are not available in the UK.

100 Series Turning Chisels   1/4"

actual size

150 Series Turning Chisels   5/16"

actual size

200 Series Turning Chisels   3/8"

actual size

Di-Accurate Sizing Chisels   1/4"

actual size

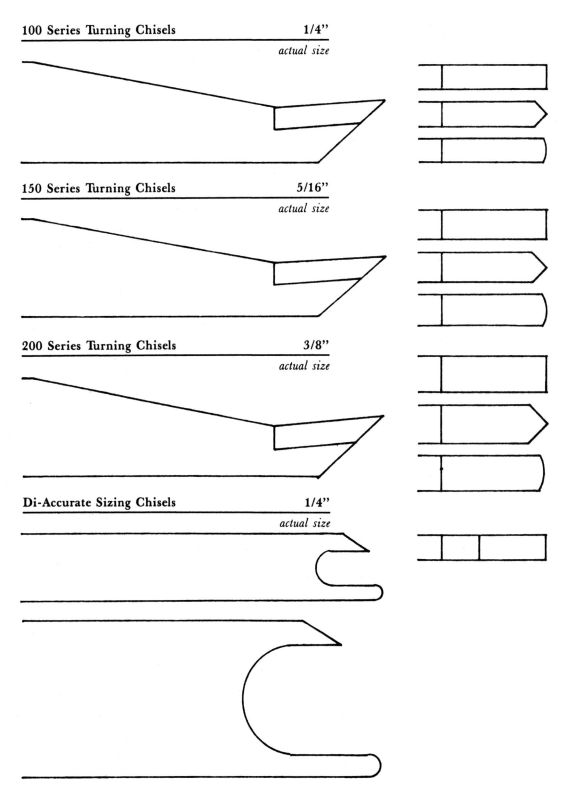

185 Arnall chisels

Some quite unusual chisels carrying the name Vega Lemco are marketed by Vega Enterprises of Decatur in Illinois (Fig 184). They were designed by the well known woodturner A. J. Lemler who lives in Sedalia in Missouri. The chisels are mainly of long and strong design with handles of maple turned by the master himself. The chisels are of low carbon steel, milled to shape with a 5% cobalt high speed steel cutting insert, silver brazed into a socket. The tools are then ground over-all and sharpened.

The chisels come in three different end shapes – square across, diamond, and radiused, with each shape available in three sizes ¼, ⁵⁄₁₆ and ³⁄₈in (6, 8 and 10mm) and in overall lengths of 18½ and 24in (472 and 610mm). The square across chisels could be used as parting tools, but a number of Di-Accurate sizing tools are listed from ³⁄₈ to 1¼in (10 to 32mm). The latter are a complete departure from the sizing tool seen on page 100, but once the technique of using them is mastered they could be extremely useful for the turner on repetitive work.

Another group of tools, which illustrate once again the dedication to perfection of the turner, are the Arnall-range (Fig 185), again made in Australia. Harry and David Arnall have tackled the problems encountered by turners working deep inside bowls and other vessels, through a very small opening. Elsewhere I have referred to this as limited aperture turning. The Arnalls have not only invented a chuck for this work (see page 85), but also a gate toolrest (see page 99), for supporting a number of tipped cutting tools. Called the gate tool set the tools are manufactured from 25 x 12mm (1 x ½in) mild steel bar and are tipped in high speed steel. The tips are attached using a special glue and the heat from an oven. They can be changed at any time and new tips mounted. There are five basic shapes; an ovoid tip dressing tool, three different sizes of hollowing tool and a boring tool. All are extremely safe to use in conjunction with the gated toolrest, which, in spite of its size, in no way restricts the operator. Obviously limited aperture turning has come to stay, and it is good to see someone tackling the tool problem. The strange thing is that most of the limited aperture tools shown in this book have very small cutting edges.

The Arnall range also includes heavy duty shaping and roughing gouges, parting tools, and a number of scrapers again tipped in HSS – tools once again from practising craftsmen.

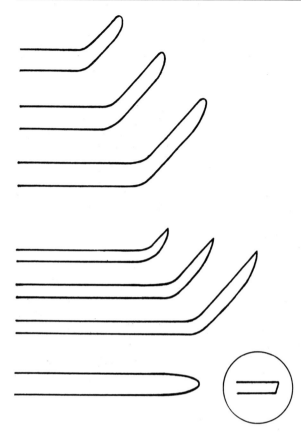

186 *Limited aperture tools similar to those of David Ellsworth*

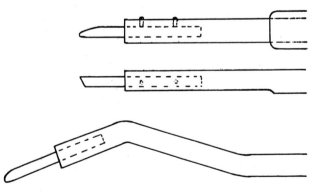

187 *Limited aperture tools with removable tips*

David Ellsworth has become a legendary turner of limited aperture work, and his delicate vessels are marvelled at by all who have been privileged to see and touch them (Figs 186, 187). The tools he uses are of his own invention, and he fashions a new one when the need arises. So far as I know they have not been produced commercially, but some shapes quite like his are shown in Fig 186. His are made in drill core steel.

Henry Taylor and Sons of Sheffield are perhaps best known for their range of carving tools. They attracted a great deal of attention when they introduced the super flute gouge designed by the Childs and made in solid high speed steel. It was suggested that this tool would supersede others and dispense with the need to have a number of bowl gouges. Most turners used the ⅜in (10mm) bowl gouge, but the super flute has become extremely popular.

Newborn Key lives at Hillboro in New Mexico; he has been turning for the best part of his life although he is a sailor by profession. His tools again illustrate that anywhere in the world where wood is turned there are men who find their own solutions to the problems they meet (Fig 188). In this way their work is enriched and our lives, also, when we hear about them.

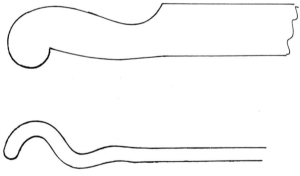

188 *The tools of Newborn Key*

Newborn regularly changes the shape of his scraping tools to suit the job of the moment, to simplify the turning, and to remove the possible hazards likely to be encountered. He makes his tools from 'found' material, often using old files and small round stock. The cutting part of each tool follows the usual round nose of the scraper, but the long sides are shaped (relieved really) on the left hand side to allow the tool to cut far inside a vessel and round the corner while the right hand side is cut away almost to follow the outside shape of the vessel around the mouth. Such shaping gives much greater freedom to move the tool on inside cuts without any danger of the tool fouling the edge or aperture of the vessel.

His round tools are extremely well thought out since the curves are made so that the cutting edge is exactly in line with the axis of the tool. This prevents the tool being tipped sideways with the rotation of the work.

The small round tools will be found most useful for tiny work. I am quite sure that Newborn has mastered the art of tempering, but anyone considering the use of such material is advised to read page 127. Certainly his work must give him the double pleasure of making tools and using them for turning.

HOOK TOOLS

These tools were used a long time ago and many people seem to think that they are very dangerous and not to be used by the novice woodturner. Holtzapfel refers to them in his catalogue of nineteenth century tools, and drawings are clearly shown in *Hand and Simple Turning – Principles and Practice*, written by John Jacob Holtzapfel in 1881, yet reference to the catalogues of the major tool manufacturers on both sides of the Atlantic elicits no information whatsoever about them. Undoubtedly they were used by many craftsmen in Europe, and we can only assume that they were made by local blacksmiths to suit particular craftsmen. These men were largely engaged in the making of domestic kitchen ware in beech and sycamore. Examples of the tools can be seen in the Welsh Museum at St Fagans in Cardiff, and those of Lalley, mentioned in H. V. Morton's *England* are happily on view at the Reading Folk Museum. Another source of information is a book published in Germany – *Das Drechslerwerk* by Fritz Spannagel.

All these tools had very small hooks, were quite long and were often bent for working three or four bowls from one block. I have seen a set of hooks under the signature of Buck (which I assume is Buck of the USA) but they were quite unlike those in the museums. For many years some of these tools have been manufactured in Scandinavia, but once again the hooks are larger than those used in the last century. Those of Hans Karlsson are unusual. The photographs show some of these (Fig 189) and on testing I

189 Tools of Hans Karlsson

have come to the conclusion that the smaller curve makes for easier and safer cutting. It is certain that the old turner did not work at the high speeds we enjoy, and we would be wise to take heed of this and keep below 800rpm when using hook tools. A good polish on the bevel helps, and once again the principle of letting the bevel rest on the wood applies. The tool must on no account be offered to the work like a begging bowl; it must be turned sideways so that the shaving is taken in a slicing cut as shown in the photographs, the tool angled at approximately 60° to the horizontal. I find it easier to work below centre, and this is emphasised by the manufacture, in Norway, of a dropped hook (see photograph). This feature helps in the correct presentation of the tool to the work.

Ed Moultrop, in the United States, uses the hook on extremely long tools to cut enormous vessels, the timber for which has to be hoisted using block and tackle. Whenever he loses a grandchild he knows where to look!

RING TOOLS

These are a variation on the hook, but consist of a perfect ring, ground both on the outside and on the inside. Sharpening is done on the inside bevel.

These are shown in the tool list of Luna (Sweden) and also in the list of Axner in Vreta Kloster. They are used exactly as the hook tool. One of the greatest exponents of this type of tool is an Australian, Vin Smith who lives at Hobart in Tasmania. He uses them for both faceplate and spindle work (Fig 190) and has brought this to a fine art. They are popular in Scandinavia, and with the spread of teaching videos it seems likely that this type of tool will be seen in increasing numbers.

With both ring and hook tools, the position of the toolrest has to be changed. A gap must be left between the face of the rest and the work. This allows for entry of the tool and its free movement over the work.

MAKING TOOLS FOR TURNING

There are many times when the turner wishes he had a tool to meet a particular problem – where the

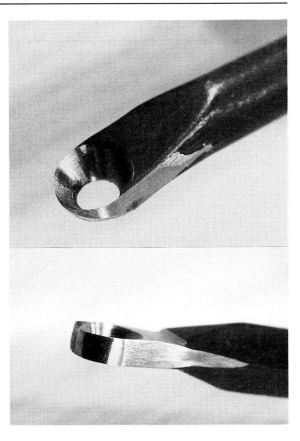

190 The ring tools of Vin Smith

standard tool is found inadequate. I have always kept a stock of round and square silver steel and flat gauge plate steel in the workshop together with old worn or useless tools. This material has often been pressed into use in making additional tools.

Straightforward shaping of small chisels and scraping tools can easily be done using the double-ended grinder.

Small gouges can be made by setting a round bar in the drill chuck or 3-jaw chuck mounted on the lathe mandrel. The 3-jaw chuck will accept longer pieces of steel that can pass through the chuck and lathe spindle. Another chuck will be needed to hold a small Slocombe drill used to make a starting hole to locate the drill chosen to give the gouge the required size of flute. The procedure is to drill very carefully, using a drop of oil to make the work easier and to keep the metal cool. After drilling to depth, slice off a little under half of the side of the rod to make the flute. Grind carefully to final shape and clean up ready for heat treatment and polishing. Small gouges can also be made by mounting an electric drill horizontally, using one of the several stands available and inserting a small grinding wheel shaped to make the flute. By passing the round rod under the wheel shaping can be carried out. This is a trifle slow but with little equipment available it is a solution. It is certainly a method useful for the miniaturist since the number of tools available for him (or her) is limited. The chisels of the carpenter and joiner can also be modified to serve as turning tools.

Many turners use old files for making scraping tools; and if this practice is followed, it must constantly be borne in mind that the steel is different from that used in wood chisels. All teeth must be ground away and full heat treatment given, otherwise the tools could shatter in use.

There are many turners, particularly miniaturists, who use nails and other small pieces of steel to make tools. The edges will not last long, but they can easily be reground and may serve their purpose well.

All workshop-made tools must be hardened and tempered before use. Occasionally it may also be necessary to re-harden tools which have had the temper drawn through overheating. Whenever steel is heated in air, oxidisation takes place and oxides appear on the surface of the metal. The oxides are of many hues, each depending on the temperature at that particular spot. The colours vary from very pale straw through various browns and purples to blue and they travel in fairly clean bands across the metal. To see the true colours clearly the metal must be bright, and the job should be done in daylight.

191 Mini-turning tools made from standard firmer chisels

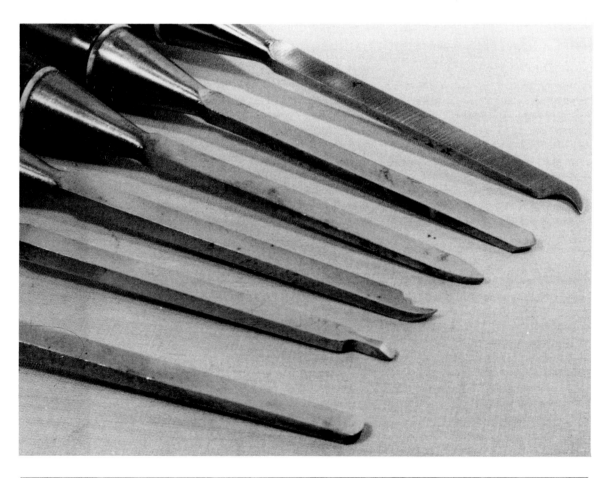

Heat can be applied in several ways – the easiest by using a blow torch which can either be the paraffin or the gas cylinder type. Alternatively, a steel tube heated over a gas ring can be used for blades small enough to go inside it. Large tools can be placed on a steel plate placed across a gas ring. A can of water or oil will also be needed to cool the tool as well as small tongs and emery cloth.

All carbon steel tools must first be hardened. Hold the tool in the flame, apply the heat about 3in (75mm) from the cutting edge, and when the metal reaches cherry red in colour the temperature will be approximately 800-850° Celsius. Quench immediately in the water or oil. Hold the tool vertically and cool it rapidly: this will ensure a good hardness (Figs 191, 192, 193).

A tool cooled in water will be much harder than one cooled in oil since oil cooling tends to be slower. Old motor oil can be used but have a good canful. A small quantity will tend to heat up rapidly and may ignite. Do not harden the complete tool otherwise the tang end will be brittle. Be careful to immerse the tool vertically into the bath to avoid distortion.

When the tool is cool, wipe it dry and use the emery cloth to polish the first couple of inches (50mm). Carefully apply the flame behind the polished area. After a short time a colour band will appear and move along the tool, away from the torch point and toward the cutting edge. When light straw appears at the edge, quench the tool very quickly to

192 *Tools made from old brass turning tools for ring cutting*

stop the edge overheating. This will give the correct temper.

Clean the tool with the emery and press on the handle. There is a simple method of changing the temper of an old file. First send your wife for a short stay with her mother, then turn on the cooker and bring the heat up to 430°F (220°C). Place the tools on a tray in the cooker and leave them for upwards of an hour. Remove them from the oven and plunge them vertically into a can of cold water – this will give them the standard wood chisel temper.

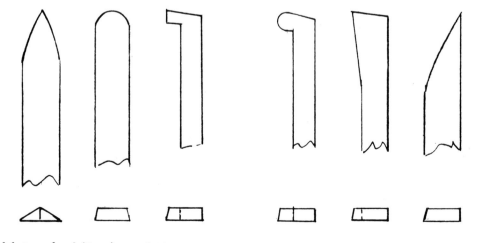

193 *Workshop made mini-turning scrapers*

TEMPERING CHART

Yellow	Pale Straw	428°F (220°C) 446°F (230°C)	For keen edges – surgeon's equipment knives
	Golden	470°F (243°C)	
Brown	Golden Purple	490°F (254°C) 510°F (265°C)	Chisels, scissors Plane irons, adzes
Purple		530°F (277°C)	All other wood-working tools
Blue	Bright Full Dark	550°F (288°C) 560°F (293°C) 600°F (315°C)	Saws and auger bits
Red	Cherry	800°F–850°F (430°C–446°C)	Softer if allowed to cool in air

Alloy steels must have very careful heat treatment or the steel may be ruined. A metallurgist should be consulted if such material needs treatment.

IDENTIFICATION OF YOUR STEEL

To identify a particular piece of steel, grind on a dry wheel. Whitish yellow sparks keeping close together indicate plain carbon steel, and dull red sparks scattering in all directions will indicate high speed steel.

TO ASCERTAIN THE HARDNESS WITHOUT THE USE OF HARDNESS MACHINES

Drop a spot of concentrated nitric acid on hard steel. This should produce a deep black spot, the lighter the spot, the softer the steel. The steel is not affected by the acid, but wash it off and wash your hands as well with plenty of water.

8

TOOLS FOR BORING

The only boring tool purposely designed for the woodturning lathe is the long hole auger. It was first made by William Ridgway in Sheffield – guided by the late Frank Pain (Fig 194).

The basic requirements with any boring tool of this kind are that it will run on centre throughout its travel and will be long enough to make the flex hole in table and floor lampstands. The bit is fluted for part of its length and has a curved lip at the centre that helps to maintain the centrality of the auger as the lifter or cutting edge forms the hole. They are available in ¼, ⁵⁄₁₆, ³⁄₈ and ⁷⁄₁₆in (6, 8, 10 and 12mm) diameter and in 30in (760mm) lengths. They are often fitted with a round handle or a round cross-handle; neither of these is satisfactory since the round one, fitted like a chisel handle, will not give sufficient grip and the latter may split if pushed too hard, with possible damage to the hand. Preferably make a handle as shown on page 147, Fig 230.

The long hole auger and the workpiece must be supported before boring can begin. There are several attachments which can be fitted to the lathe to provide a support for the timber (in place of the running or dead centre) and at the same time allow the auger to be passed through. The simplest of these is a hollow centre that replaces the tailstock centre with the timber running on a tiny rim. Adjustment of the centre into the timber is made using the tailstock advancing mechanism. They are available in Nos 1 and 2 Morse taper – Fig 195.

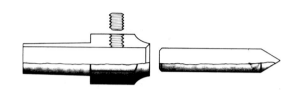

195 Long hole boring attachment

AVAILABLE SIZES

⁵⁄₁₆″ bore with No. 1 Morse taper shank
³⁄₈″ bore with No. 1 Morse taper shank
⁵⁄₁₆″ bore with No. 2 Morse taper shank
³⁄₈″ bore with No. 2 Morse taper shank

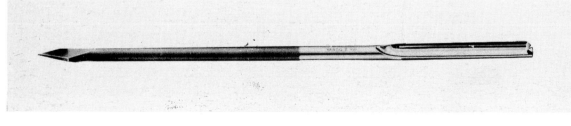

194 Long hole boring auger

196 Harrison tailstock boring attachment

The Harrison Company makes two, one of which fits over the sleeve of the tailstock (Fig 196). It has a rim and is available for several sizes of auger. The other fits into the tool-/hand-rest base, is held in place by the toolrest locking lever, and can be adjusted into the workpiece by turning the tailstock barrel, which is locked by a screw at the top (Fig 197). It is accurately centred by bringing up the tailstock centre.

Both Myford and Coronet have one similar to the Harrison but with the addition of a centring pin (Fig 198). Elu has a running centre, with a removable point enabling it to be converted to a long hole boring centre. All the foregoing will accept auger sizes of ⁵⁄₁₆ and ³⁄₈in (8 and 10mm) (Fig 199).

197 Harrison attachment fits in place of the toolrest

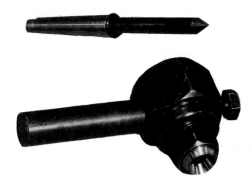

198 Coronet long hole boring attachment with guide pin

199 Elu tailstock running centre, with removable pin to enable the boring tool to be passed through

200 Long hole boring attachment in use.

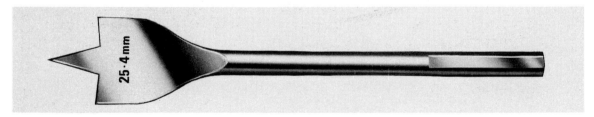

201 Flatbit

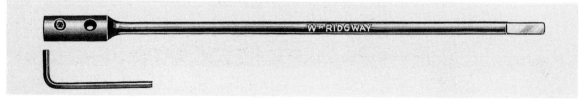

202 Flatbit extension

Care must be exercised when using the auger. It must be removed frequently to allow the waste to fall out. If the flute is filled with chips there is a danger that the work may burst or the auger run off centre (Fig 200).

Holes up to 1½in (38mm) can be bored using the spade type bit. These are speedy and accurate, but care must be exercised in use, since, if pushed too hard into the work they can run with the grain and thus go off-centre. They should also run at high speed, and the brad point must be located in the wood before starting up. The flatbit, in Fig 201, is a typical example, having a long brad point with forward and side cutting edges angled to form a point at the periphery of the hole. The hole is planed whereas the auger cuts and lifts. The spadebit shank has three flats for accurate location in the drill chuck; the flats are usually longer than the chuck is deep – this will stop the bit moving back into the chuck. The flatbit can be fitted with an extension for holes of greater depth; the diameter of the small chuck at the end of the extension will not allow the smaller bits to be used. There are several types of spadebit in use with slight variations in shape (Fig 202).

Although not specifically designed for use on the lathe, the sawtooth machine bit (multi-spur bit in the USA) has become a firm favourite with the turner. It bores in soft or hardwood, its ripsaw-like teeth scribe the periphery of the hole and its two cutters or lifters cut, lift, and pass the shavings out of the escapement of the bit. These bits bore very accurate holes as deep as their length will allow. The small sizes should be withdrawn frequently throughout a deep bore to remove the waste, since there is a real danger of the shavings building up behind the bit and preventing its withdrawal. They are splendid for boring out waste as well as for the accurate boring of boxes, vases and similar work (Fig 203). Sizes are available between ⅜ and 3½in (10 and 90mm).

The Forstner bit is really the tool of the cabinet maker and patternmaker, but it can be used for lathe work. These bits should never cut holes greater in depth than twice their diameter, since there is a great danger of burning both tool and work. The bit runs on its finely machined periphery, and a slow speed with a fast rate of feed is needed to avoid burning. This bit will be found ideal when cutting recesses for inlay work. Sizes from ⅜ to 3½in (10 to 90mm) are available (Fig 204).

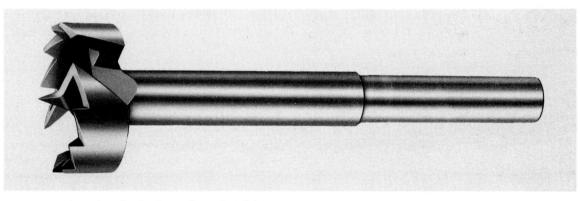

203 Sawtooth machine bit (Multispur bit in the USA)

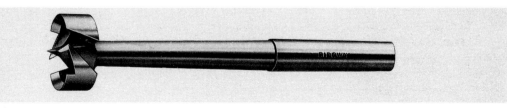

204 Forstner bit

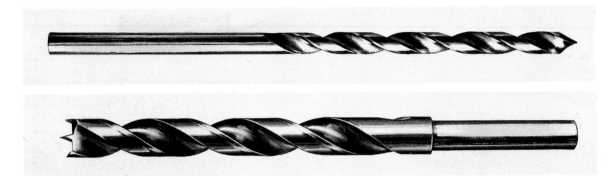

The single twist bit, often called a super spur bit, has been given new life in recent times. It has a screw point which serves to wind the bit into the work while the shavings or chips move out through the twist. The screw point was a feature in the days when most wood machines ran at slow speeds which ensured the quick movement of the tool into the work. Today, when the reverse is the case, this bit is best used with the screw filed to a brad point to prevent too rapid entry into the workpiece. They are available in a range of imperial and metric sizes.

205 Wood drill
206 Lip and spur bit

Small holes can be made using the wood drill, which is similar in design to the engineer's twist drill but has a more open flute and a longer pointed nose helping to give instant location of the bit. Fig 205 shows the drill which is available in sizes up to ½in (12mm).

The lip and spur bit is similar to the drill, but it has a brad point and two lifters. It bores very easily and very accurately. Sizes up to ½in (12mm) are available (Fig 206).

For lamp-standard work, where the standard is made up in two or three sections, a counter-boring tool is needed to cut a round mortice to receive a round tenon, which can be made during the turning of the standard. This tool comprises a 1in (25mm) 4-prong counter-boring bit (rather like a very sharp 4-prong driving centre) with an interchangeable parallel pilot or pointed centre. The other end has a Morse taper (Fig 207). After the long hole boring tool has been used to make a hole halfway along the length of the workpiece, the work is removed and the driving fork replaced at the headstock with the counter-boring tool fitted with the parallel point. The work is reversed with the bored hole located on the pin, the prongs located in the recesses cut by the

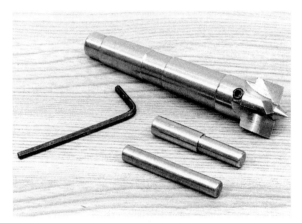

207 Counter-boring tool with interchangeable pilot

driving centre. The long hole boring attachment is utilised, and the hole boring completed. A recess can then be cut by winding up the tailstock – the counter-boring tool will cut on centre and to the depth required to receive the tenon. With the centre point in position the tool can be used as a driving fork.

There are several designs of plug cutters. Those which eject the plug through the side are best, but those which cut a single plug are fairly cheap. They will cut plugs for inlay work, while the miniaturist will find them useful to cut blanks for tiny workpieces. They are available in sizes from ¼ up to 3in (6 to 75mm) (Fig 208). The work must be held securely since the plug cutter has no centre on which to run.

A number of bits can be made from flatbits by regrinding (Fig 209).

208 Plug cutters

209 Flatbits reshaped

210 Expanding machine bit

211 Drill jig and bushes

Several types of the expanding machine bit are available and many are extremely expensive. The one shown (Fig 210) is made in Germany and bores holes up to 35mm (1⅜in) in diameter. The turner is advised to run the machine on slow speed and be careful to clear the bit of shavings frequently. This is particularly important when deep boring, otherwise the shavings may pile up behind the bit, making withdrawal difficult.

A drill chuck is an essential part of the lathe equipment, and it must be fitted with a Morse taper arbor to suit the bore of the lathe. The chuck should have a capacity of ½in (12mm) since most machine bits have ½in (12mm) shanks. Coronet has a chuck which can be screwed to the headstock spindle of its machines to serve as an excellent chuck for holding small work. Fitted with a screwed Morse taper mandrel it can be used in the tailstock (see page 91).

A useful tool is the drill jig which can be fitted in place of the toolrest in the banjo or tool-/hand-rest base. It will receive a ¾in (20mm) drill without a drill bush, but drill bushes of ¼, ⅜ and ½in (6, 10 and 12mm) are available. They are useful for drilling holes in the base of lamp standards, after turning on the headstock; holes for plug decoration; and any hole which has to be drilled in faceplate work (Fig 211).

9

EQUIPMENT THAT CAN BE MADE

THE GLUE CHUCK (Fig 212)

This is one of the most useful methods of holding yet devised. Years ago, the standard method of holding blocks for woodturning, where the turner objected to unsightly holes in the base of the job, was to screw a block of waste timber to a faceplate, turn the face flat, apply a thin film of glue, then a piece of brown paper followed by another film of glue and finally the workpiece. The assembly was then clamped up and left for the glue to dry. Truly a time wasting procedure. When the job was completed the joint had to be broken at the paper and the glue cleaned off.

One way I devised to avoid this, particularly with small pieces of timber, was to use double-sided tape. This has now become a standard method with many turners and is certainly taught by a good friend on the other side of the Atlantic. My most-used method is one about which several people have expressed doubt, but it has been used by others for many years. A waste block is screwed to a faceplate or screwchuck and its face made perfectly flat. The workpiece is prepared with one of its faces also perfectly flat.

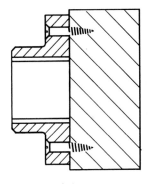

212 Glue chuck.

A very thin film of glue from a hot-melt glue gun is spread over the face of the waste wood block. The workpiece is positioned and the whole clamped together, working quite quickly, using either a C clamp set to the approximate throat size (in the interest of speed) or a bench vice. Turning can commence immediately, and when the job is completed a thin knife tapped in at the glue line separates the two. I use a long thin cobbler's knife for this and tap with a hammer. Usually the break comes easily since glue is only on the chuck. Should difficulty be experienced, warm the knife. Another alternative is to use hot air – this can come from a hair drier (don't let your wife catch you) or from a paint remover.

The glue chuck can be used repeatedly even without the addition of new glue. It can be rewarmed using the hot air. With attention to facing and to the amount of glue used (don't put on too much, otherwise it acts like a cushion and the work may wobble) it can be used to hold quite large pieces.

THE WOOD CHUCK (Fig 213)

This is an old and well-tried method and one which can be used when all else seems impossible. A wastewood block is screwed to a faceplate and a recess is cut of diameter equal to the size of the work. The recess has a slight taper to assist in holding. The turning of the underside of, say, a plate can be completed, including the edge. It is then taken off the lathe (it would probably have been held on a screwchuck) and inverted into the recess. Then the inside can be turned. Alternatively, a disc can be turned of exact size to fit the chuck and the edge finalised at this stage. The complete turning can then be carried out in the chuck. Work which can have a small plinth

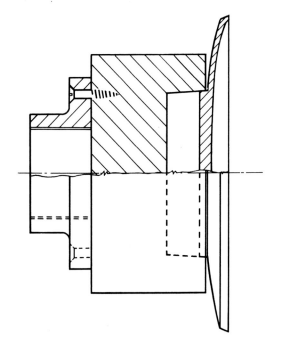

213 Wood chuck

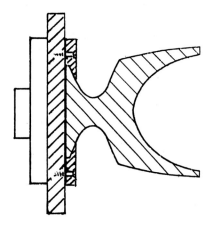

214 Two-part wood chuck with removable face

cut on the underside can also be held in the wood chuck.

A variation of this applies where the job has a small foot at the base. Here a piece is screwed to the faceplate and another block cut into four quarters is screwed to it. A recess is cut in this and undercut to receive the foot shape. Two adjacent sections are removed, the job pushed into place, and the segments replaced. This provides a safe and positive location (Fig 214).

This type of chuck, in deeper form, can be used to hold spherical work for completion after part turning between centres. Some professional turners use this idea for finishing work which has been held on the screwchuck or the faceplate. To eliminate the holes, the bowl or box is reversed into a prepared recess – a fairly close fit is needed – then the underside is turned to remove the holes.

A drill chuck, into which is fitted a small wood dowel, is placed in the tailstock. The job is inserted into a recess, which in this case is merely a means of centring. The dowel is brought up to hold the work in place and careful cutting will remove all but the tiny piece under the dowel. This can be cut away with a small knife after completion of the whole.

CHUCK FOR DOOR AND DRAWER KNOBS

Small knobs are usually turned between centres in a stick, then parted off. Unfortunately, the little parting cut will show on the top of each knob. A small block attached to a faceplate or a screwchuck can be bored to receive the little tenon left at the end of each knob for insertion in the piece of furniture. The knobs can be pushed into this little chuck and completed without problems.

THE WOOD DOG CHUCK (Fig 215)

This is a method of holding used by the engineer; he has specially designed faceplates in which dogs can slide and be screwed up tightly to secure the work. An adaptation of this idea uses a disc screwed to a faceplate. The face is turned flat, and a number of circles of known diameter are marked out on this face using a sharp point. These will serve as guides for accurate placement of the job during assembly. Four

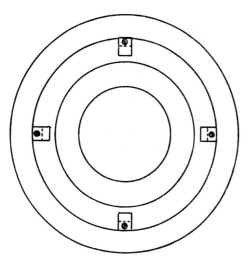

215 Wood dog chuck

dogs are made, these can be shaped to fit over the job or can have a simple rebate cut in them at the forward end. If a bowl requires facing on its underside to remove the screw holes, or a plate needs finishing on one side, this method of holding will be found satisfactory. The job is accurately centred using the marked circles. The dogs are positioned and tightened, using holes cut in the dogs beforehand. This method can also be used for turning an offset inside part of plates and dishes.

WOODEN MANDRELS (Fig 216)

Mandrels can be used for completing partly turned work, where partial cutting has produced a recess or where work is carried out on pre-bored timber.

A mandrel is a means of holding timber firmly for turning, permitting the completed job to be removed easily. Where the mandrel is to be in constant use, it will be best in a good long-grained hardwood free from knots, but for the odd job soft waste timber

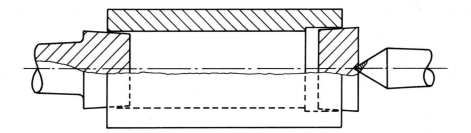

216 Plug mandrels

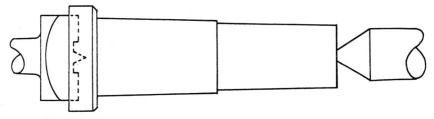

217 Serviette ring mandrel

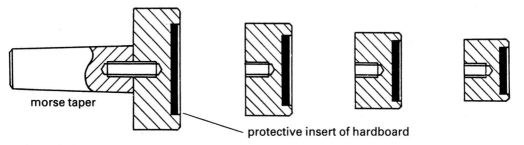

morse taper

protective insert of hardboard

218 Metal mandrel with removable heads

will suffice. A mandrel used for turning serviette and other rings can become a permanent part of the workshop equipment (Fig 217). Mandrels can also be used for holding boxes, to enable the underside to be finished. The block can be held on a faceplate and once again a very slight taper cut to ensure a good fit.

A multi-use mandrel made in aluminium and screwed to a Morse taper is shown in Fig 218. Four sizes proved most useful for holding small boxes and tiny picture frames.

PLUG MANDRELS (Fig 219)

A popular method of making pepper and salt mills is to bore the inside of the mill material first. A small piece of wood is placed between centres and turned to make two tapered plugs, one for each end of the bored material; the one at the headstock has a Morse taper to suit the lathe. The taper need not be exact, but it should be a good fit. The mills are easily mounted and turned to completion. These plugs can be used many times.

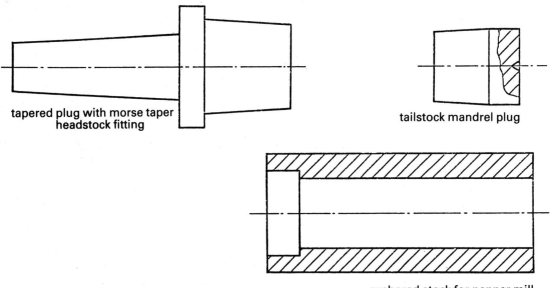

tapered plug with morse taper
headstock fitting

tailstock mandrel plug

prebored stock for pepper mill

219 Plug mandrels for pre-bored work – headstock – taper plug with Morse taper fitting – tailstock mandrel plug – prepared stock for pepper mill

SIMPLE DEPTH GAUGE (Fig 220)

A depth gauge can be a most useful tool, yet these are not made for the woodturner. A simple one can be made from a strip of planed timber ¾ x ¼ x 12in (20 x 6 x 305mm) long. At the centre a ¼in (6mm) hole is drilled to receive a dowel. Measurements can be placed on the dowel, or the depth read off using a rule. The strip is laid across the face of the bowl, the dowel pushed through until it registers in the bottom of the bowl, then withdrawn so that the depth can be read off.

An improved version made in steel in school has been in use in my workshop for many years. The steel pin is held in a tiny collet and fixed by turning the collar (Fig 221).

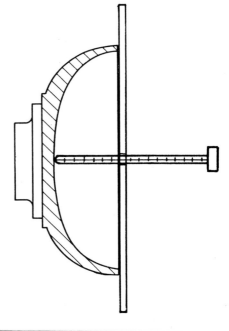

220 Simple depth gauge

221 Adjustable bowl depth gauge made in mild steel

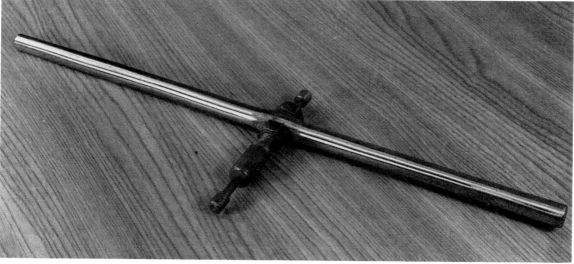

SUPPORTING PIECES FOR THE RUNNING CENTRE (Fig 222)

When making goblets and similar work, the usual practice is to complete the cutting of the bowl before tackling the stem and base. This ensures that, during the heavier cutting of the inside, there will be plenty of support from the surrounding timber. At the same time a little problem arises when turning the stem of the vessel – particularly if this should be of slender form; the work needs to be supported at the bowl end to guard against accidents.

A method much used is to turn a disc which fits snugly just inside the lip of the bowl. The disc has an accurate centre cut in it, and the running centre is brought up to support it inside the bowl.

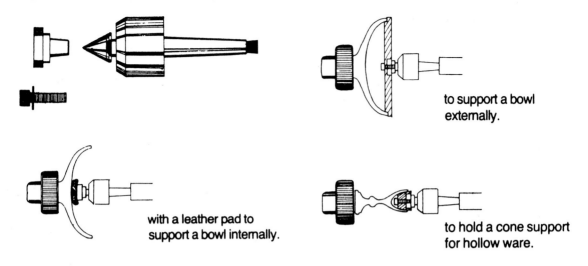

to support a bowl
externally.

with a leather pad to
support a bowl internally.

to hold a cone support
for hollow ware.

222 Supporting pieces for the running centre

With the introduction of the multi-purpose running centre one of the components parts is screwed to receive a threaded bolt. This in turn holds the prepared disc, converting it to a running disc centre. The one shown is part of the Craft Supplies deluxe running centre.

DRAW BOLT AND PLUG

Work having a centre hole can be secured to the headstock for limited turning using a draw bolt and plug. This comprises a threaded rod (studding can be used) of length sufficient to pass through the headstock. A prepared tapered plug is fitted and nuts and bolts added. The turning can be assembled quickly; it centres automatically and is ideal for wheels for toys and similar items.

WHEEL CHUCK

For the 'once only' job of turning wheels a piece of timber attached to a faceplate can be turned to a diameter slightly less in size than the wheels. The wheel material can be screwed to this and each side cut in turn. Obviously, with repeated use there would be a serious loss of centricity in using the wood screw.

CHUCK FOR SQUARE STOCK

Square stock can be accurately and safely driven using a block screwed to a faceplate. The block has a square hole cut it in of exact size of the material to be turned; the hole must of course be perfectly centred.

SQUEEZE CHUCK WITH CLIP FOR ADJUSTMENT (Fig 223)

This chuck will be found useful for holding small boxes, lids, rings, vases and other partly turned work. I made one many years ago to solve the problem of holding lids which were needed for kitchen spice bottles.

Choose a fairly close-grained hardwood for this job if it is to be put to a considerable amount of use, otherwise softwood will do. The piece is turned to size and an annular groove cut around the outside close to the front of the chuck. When the turning is complete remove it from the lathe and make two cuts with the tenon saw at right angles to each other, across the face of the chuck, and to a depth of two thirds the total depth of the chuck recess.

Place a Jubilee-type hose clip in the recess; the wire type will also do. This clip, when tightened with a screwdriver, will help to squeeze the sides down sufficiently to hold the job securely. The recess should be cut deep enough to house the clip completely. A screw standing proud could be injurious to the hand. Slight inaccuracies in measurement either

223 Squeeze chuck with hose clip adjustment

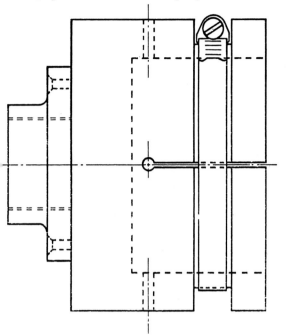

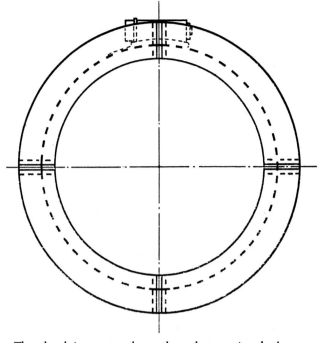

way will be accommodated in the adjustment possible with this chuck.

SPLIT CHUCK WITH SQUEEZE COLLAR (Fig 224)

This is very like the Jubilee clip chuck, but uses a wood or metal ring to squeeze the jaws together.

The chuck is prepared exactly as that previously described, but the outside is tapered to receive the ring. The chuck is cut with the saw. A wooden ring can be turned separately using a piece of strong closely-grained hardwood mounted on a screw-chuck. A metal ring would be better, and a suitable one should be obtained before the chuck is turned.

224 Split chuck with squeeze collar

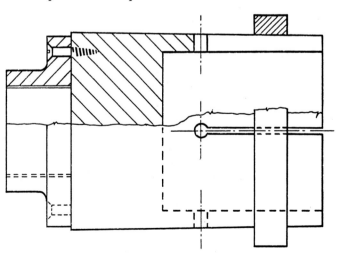

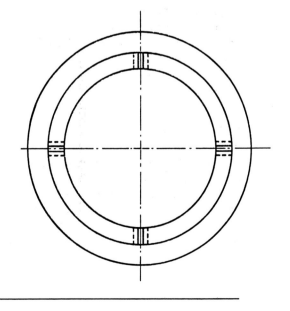

HANDLE MANDREL

When making mallets for carving or mauls for stone laying or similar mallets, the handle itself can be used as the mandrel. Turn the handle, first cutting a tenon at the tailstock end. Bore a blank for the mallet head and slide this over the turned tenon; the fit should be good so that the block does not spin round during the turning. The job can be completed, polished if necessary, and when removed from the lathe, the head can be pushed off to permit the cutting of a tapered slot in the tenon for the insertion of wedges when the job is finally assembled.

WHEEL JIG AS AN ADDITION TO THE PRECISION COMBINATION CHUCK (Fig 225, 226)

Some of the components of the combination chuck have a No 3 Morse taper at one end to house them in the centre boss. I turned such a taper, tapped it to

225 Wheel jig for precision combination chuck

226 Wheel jig assembled in the chuck

receive a Whitworth screw at the smaller diameter and to receive the chuck screw at the other – which enables it to be held securely in the Morse taper. Into the other end is screwed a piece of studding long enough to receive the woodblanks with a securing screw and washer. This makes a fine addition to the chuck. Alternatively, it could be made in wood, but it would only have a very limited life.

LATHE STEADY (Fig 227)

Most steadies offered by manufacturers for the wood lathe are usually a modification of those used on metalwork lathes and are not really very satisfactory since the supporting fingers bear on the timber, have to be constantly adjusted, and end up by burning the job.

Years ago I made the one shown ıor a Myford lathe, and this proved satisfactory. The wheels revolved with the job, and the spring loaded arm kept the wheels in constant contact. This idea has been taken a step further in a design shown on page 104.

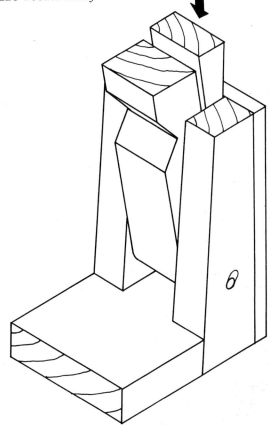

228 Wooden steady

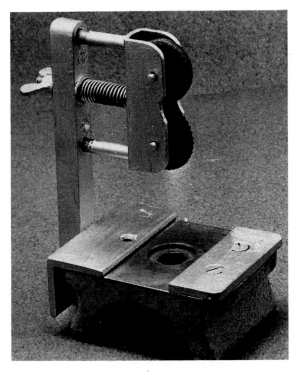

227 Steady designed for the Myford ML8 lathe

WOOD STEADY (Fig 228)

The traditional method of supporting thin work was to make a steady fitted with a wedge which dropped down into a recess at the rear to keep an arm in contact with the revolving work. This worked well enough but constant reference had to be made to the assembly to avoid burning. With this type of steady, cutting at the point of contact was not possible, the small section in contact being removed on completion of the cutting by supporting the workpiece with the fingers of the left hand placed behind the revolving job.

WOOD WASHERS

Plywood washers turned in a number of sizes and thicknesses will be found most useful to add to the screwchuck to reduce the amount of penetration of the screw into the workpiece. Larger ones can be used to support thin work such as picture frames turned to a thin section.

WOOD DISCS

Wood discs drilled and screwed to the precision combination chuck in the screwchuck mode, or, alternatively, having faceplate rings attached and held in the expanding dovetail jaws, can have a sheet of abrasive glued to them and be used as sanding discs for finishing the bases of jobs. Another method is to use a suitable aluminium oxide disc which will provide a means of sharpening and grinding. The wheel jig page 144 could also be used for this.

ABRASIVE SPINDLES (Fig 229)

Any number of spindles can be turned, covered with abrasive paper and either used mounted in a drill chuck placed in the headstock, or held in the hand

229 Abrasive spindles and abrasive board

with the job running in the lathe. These can be used for limited cleaning up of rings and other hollow work where access during the actual turning was impossible or limited.

ABRASIVE BOARDS

These are simply small sheets of plywood to which a sheet of abrasive paper has been glued. They are ideal for cleaning up the bases of finished articles coming off the glue chuck or similar workholding devices. This is much easier and cheaper than using unsupported sheets of paper on the bench top. A number can be made – indeed, have a library of them. They can also be built with an upstand to avoid accidents to the finished piece.

LONG HOLE BORING AUGER HANDLE (Fig 230)

A problem arises in using this tool because it tends, when pushed into the work, to revolve with the job if not well held. Usually the tool is supplied with a round handle which does not help. A wooden

230 Long bole boring auger handle

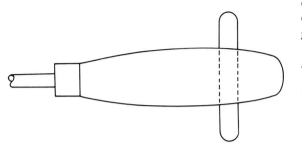

handle, turned to suit the hand of the user, then drilled so that a cross handle can be inserted, is easily the best solution. The cross handle serves to give adequate grip to resist the rotation.

MANDRELS (Figs 231, 232)

The 2in (50mm) collet in the chucks can be used to house various types of mandrels. A good quality straight-grained hardwood should be used – beech, sycamore or ash – some of mine are made of box.

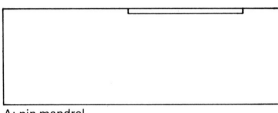

A: pin mandrel

B: taper mandrels for boxes and rings

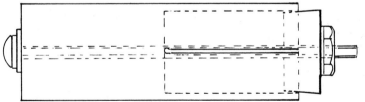

C: expanding mandrel

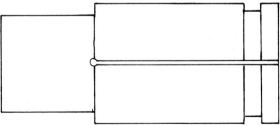

D: chuck with hose clip adjuster

231 Mandrels for the precision combination chuck used in the collet mode

E: small knob chuck

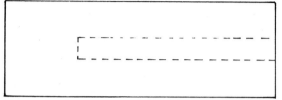

F: pen chuck

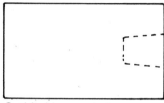

G: thimble mandrel

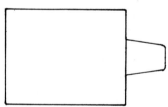

H: thimble mandrel

232 More mandrels

Turned between centres, and designed to be held without any additional support at the tailstock end, they can solve many a difficult problem.

Pin mandrels in various sizes, turned when needed and usually in the sizes not available commercially, are shown in Fig A.

Mandrels with tapers to hold boxes, rings, and serviette rings are shown in Fig B.

An expanding mandrel with a tapered wedge to provide expansion is easily made, and a screwed bolt used to provide the action. It is important to use a timber which has long, straight grain, with

sufficient strength, since the chuck will need to be split for part of its length, and the wedging action will tend to aggravate this. Very little expansion is needed to hold small rings and other pieces which have been bored internally. The expansion can also be achieved by bringing up the tailstock fitted with the solid centre (Fig C).

Fig D shows split and bored mandrels made to receive small work and function like the bigger squeeze chuck.

Another useful chuck to receive small knobs and other objects left with a spigot for holding in a press fit hole is shown in Fig 232, E and F, where a hole has been drilled in the end of the mandrel.

MANDREL FOR LADIES' THIMBLES (Fig 232, G and H)

There are many thimble collections, some in ceramics, others in ivory and silver, and quite a number in timber. Indeed, there are several collections of timber specimens which use the thimble to display beauty of colour and grain and make a refreshing change from the traditional.

There are several methods of turning thimbles and the simplest I have tried is to bore out the inside first, then mount the work on a small mandrel turned to receive it and hold it quite firmly while turning down to a thin wall.

A flatbit can quite easily be re-ground to the exact size needed for boring the inside of the thimble. The bit can be ground on the fine wheel of the double-ended grinder. First make a small pattern in paper and glue this to the face of the flatbit and then grind away the surplus metal. Have a can of water nearby for cooling; be careful to match the cutting angles and to reduce the brad point to leave only a fraction for centring.

The length of the shank of the bit can be reduced since it will not be needed for deep boring. Grind the three flats which locate the bit in the 3-jaw chuck and prevent rotation. Make the flats slightly longer than the depth of the chuck. This will ensure positive location.

The mandrel can be made from any close-grained hardwood. Turned between centres, it can be held in one or other of the chucks. For preference, and particularly if it is to be used repeatedly, it should be sized to be held in a collet. A template should be made in stiff card to check for size and shape. Another mandrel could also be made and bored out with the thimble bit to serve as a chuck to hold the workpiece if the inside needs attention.

TOOL RACKS

The housing of the tools is most important, and some care should be given to the design of the tool storage rack. Tools are best housed in racks which are easy of access and the working ends should be clearly visible to save time. The rack should support the tool safely, for preference with the business end upwards. An open base will allow shavings to clear; and is best made from triangular or round section material to facilitate this. For the convenience of my students I have used racks which can be wheeled

into position alongside the lathe and stored away when not in use. These have the tools suspended, handle upwards, so that the edges are protected but easily visible (Fig 233).

CHUCK GUARDS

A guard for the 3-/4-jaw chuck is essential, or for any chuck where the jaws extend beyond the periphery. Fig 234 shows one made from a plastic paint container and one from sheet aluminium. These can be attached to the belt guard cover of the Tyme Cub and Avon machines enabling the guard to be raised to give access to the chuck. Other lathes, which may not be equipped in this way, can be fitted with guards attached to the lathe bed or the headstock casting. Since the guard will not always be in use it should have a simple method of attachment.

233 Tool racks

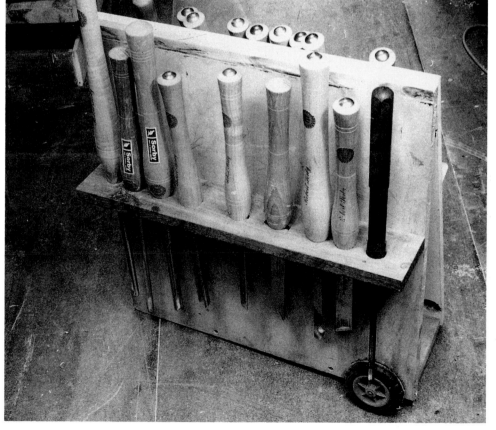

234 Chuck guards   *235 Knock-out rod*

KNOCK-OUT ROD

Many lathes are supplied with knock-out bars or rods for the removal of the centres. These rods are often far too light to do the job well. An ideal one can be made from the simple rod supplied by adding a knob. This can be turned on the lathe and bored out so that lead weight can be added. The rod can be glued in place with Araldite or similar fast-setting and gap-filling glue (Fig 235).

CHUCK FOR SQUARE PICTURE FRAMES (Fig 236)

The holding of square flats can present a problem when the centre of the workpiece has to be cut away at some time during turning. If a number of picture frames have to be turned, or this type of chuck will be needed from time to time, then it should be made from a suitable hardwood. Prepare the piece for assembly to one of the expanding collet chucks by cutting a dovetail recess. Mount it on the chuck, turn to round, and face it carefully. Make four screw blocks, and mark out the face of the timber accu-

236 Chuck for square picture frames

237 Boring jig

rately. The diagonals of the square extended to the circumference will help to position prepared square blanks, and the screwed blocks will keep the workpiece in place during turning.

BORING JIGS

Holes often need to be bored at an angle – the three-legged stool is an example where the legs are angled into the top. A hinged table, with a peg at the rear to position it in the tailstock, has been found satisfactory. The screw is actioned to set the angle and works through a threaded insert. The workpiece can be held on the hinged board with double-sided tape (Fig 237).

To bore holes in round stock with the boring tool held in the drill chuck driven by the lathe is a simple matter if a small jig is made with a vee-cut to house the work and a tapered pin at the rear is used to hold the jig.

FACEPLATE LEVER (Fig 238)

Often, when large work has been held on the faceplate, some difficulty is experienced in removing the faceplate. There are various ways of doing this that I never wish to see again – I'm a gentle man really. A lever can easily be made from a piece of steel bar, bored and tapped to receive two pins of the same diameter as the screw holes in the faceplate, and the same distance apart as the outermost of those. Rivets could be used but may be too soft. Two

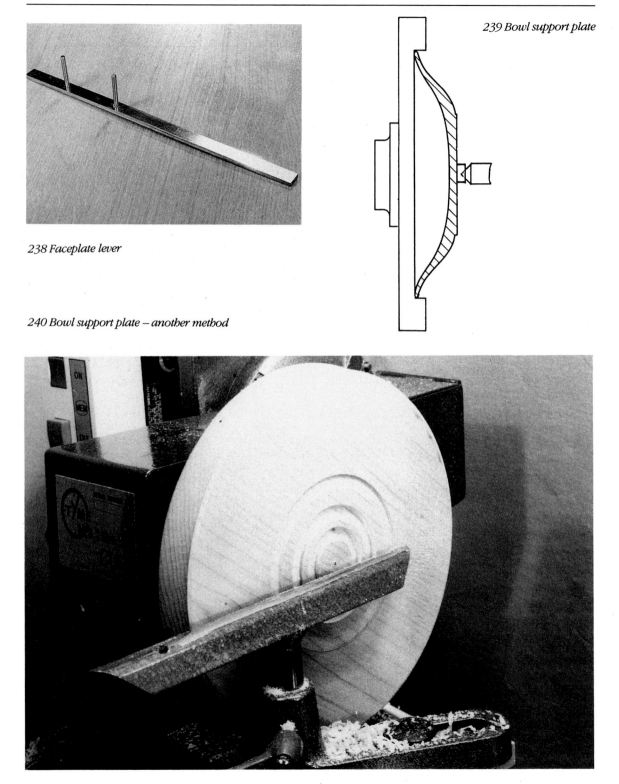

238 Faceplate lever

239 Bowl support plate

240 Bowl support plate – another method

larger holes could be bored in the faceplate if greater strength is needed. My method of removing troublesome assemblies, where a lever of this kind cannot be used, is to employ a plumber's chain wrench. This is small and designed for fitting the immersion heaters in hot water tanks. (One of these, the Record 240, has hung alongside my lathe for many years.)

BOWL SUPPORT PLATES

Where work has been held on a temporary spigot or may need attention after the bowl has been finished, a faceplate support can be used. This is simply a disc with a groove of size equal to the outside diameter of the bowl. This locates the bowl centrally when the tailstock, which will support the bowl at the base, is brought into position. If the plate is designed to be held on the expanding jaws of the combination chuck, it can be used many times and different grooves cut in it to house different sizes of bowl. A small wood plug should be placed between the running centre and the base of the bowl if the last cut is to be carried through to the centre (Figs 239, 240).

When marking out before cutting the recess for

the jaws of the expanding collet chuck, or for any similar need, a very simple tool can be made using a strip of hardwood bored to receive two round headed nails. This acts like a pair of compasses and the marking nail can be sharpened with a file to improve its performance (Fig 241).

Where recesses are constantly being cut and

241 Recess marking device

242 Gauges in plastic, wood and sheet aluminium

checked for accuracy, a gauge made from sheet plastic will be found most useful and much more convenient and time saving than calipers. I use a number of these which match the popular sizes of chuck jaws. Alternatively, one can be turned and given a little knob for holding. One for eggcups and goblets may also be helpful (Fig 242).

A gauge of sheet aluminium can be used to check spigots cut for insertion in the chuck or on handles to receive ferrules.

When mounting a workpiece onto a mandrel, or inserting it into a woodchuck, it is advisable to use a push plate mounted in the tailstock to push the work into place to ensure accuracy. Many turners use a block of wood placed across the face of the work, bringing the tailstock up to pressure the job into place but the pushplate simplifies this (Fig 243).

When drilling the hole in a table lamp to bring the flex through the base, the lathe sanding table, p104 Fig 157 can replace the toolrest, and the lamp base placed on it at the required height. The drill is set up in a chuck housed in the headstock and the work pushed onto it by sliding the unit along the lathe bed.

243 Push plate

244 A ticketer

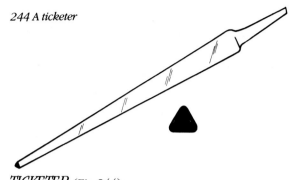

TICKETER (Fig 244)

A ticketer for turning the edge on scraping tools can be made from a worn 3-corner file. Choose one about 4in (100mm) long. Grind away all the teeth, then carefully remove the long corners rolling each one over to form a radiused edge, which will consolidate the tool material, and finally turn the hook. Polish the long edges.

STEPPED ABRASIVE WHEEL FOR GRINDING AND SHARPENING

A disc of wood can be turned and stepped down on the lathe or alternatively several discs of differing diameters can be glued and screwed together. They can be bored to receive either an adaptor for use in the electric drill or a similar type fitted on a motor spindle. The steps can carry different grades of abrasive paper for grinding and sharpening.

HORIZONTAL SHARPENER WITH A RUBBERISED ABRASIVE WHEEL

A housing can be made for a small electric motor with belt drive to a spindle carrying a rubberised wheel. The one in Fig 266 (see p168) uses a small shaft running in a simple bearing. The speed should be around 300rpm. These wheels require no lubricant or coolant.

SPEED REDUCER

Where an electric drill is being used with abrasive discs for grinding and sharpening or with a tool like

245 Speed controller

the Tantec (see page 162), a reduction in speed is needed. The electronic drill is the best answer but, where this is not possible, the turner may care either to make or to have made a simple reducer using the circuit detailed in Figs 245, 246.

PIN GUIDES

These can easily be made from thin plywood and fine panel pins transfer measurements to the workpiece from a drawing. They are also useful for repetition work (Fig 247).

Drill Speed Controller

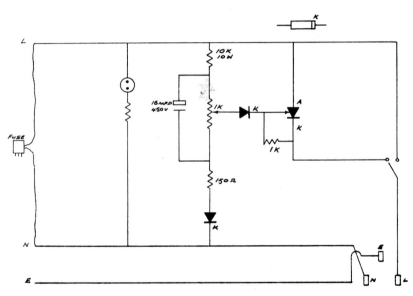

246 Controller circuitry

1 3A 250v c/o TOGGLE SWITCH.
1 NEON (240v)
2 DIODES IW4004 (400v /A)
1 WIREWOUND RESISTOR (10K 10watt)
1 ELECTROLYTIC CAPACITOR
        (16 MFD / 450v)
1 STANDARD WIREWOUND V/C
        (1 K 3 watts)
1 RESISTOR (1 K ½watt)
1 RESISTOR (150 Ω ½ watt)
1 THYRISTOR CRS 3/40
        (400v 3A)
1 13A SWITCH SOCKET
1 13A PLUG TOP
1 5A FUSE

N.B.
HEAT SINK NEEDED ON THYRISTOR.
THIS IS ALWAYS AT 240V.
DO NOT BOLT THROUGH TOP PANEL.

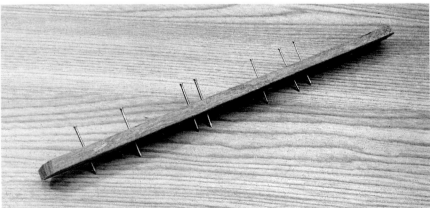

247 Pin guide

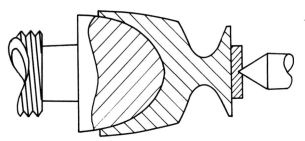

248 Eggcup mandrel

EGGCUP MANDREL

This is turned with a Morse taper to fit into the headstock spindle and used to clean up and shape the base of eggcups after parting off. The small plug is turned away at the same time leaving a minute pip to cut off with a knife when the turning is removed (Fig 248).

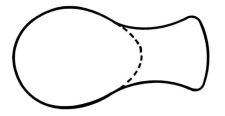

249 Eggcup template

EGGCUP TEMPLATE

A template can be made from a piece of plywood or aluminium sheeting (Fig 249).

250 Short toolrest with checkpost

SHORT TOOLREST WITH CHECK POST

Should the turner have access to welding or brazing equipment, a toolrest can easily be made of length to suit the work. The one shown is made from steel tube and mild steel rod. The check post I had turned locally (Fig 250).

10

EQUIPMENT FOR TOOL MAINTENANCE

GRINDING AND SHARPENING

There are various schools of thought about the sharpening of tools and the equipment used. The methods can be divided into:
1 sharpening by grinding only, on a fast double ended grinder
2 traditional grinding and sharpening using a grindstone followed by sharpening on an oilstone
3 grinding, sharpening and stropping (polishing)
4 grinding with sharpening and polishing in one operation.

Different types of tool may need different treatment and can be divided into:
a tools for cutting
b tools for cutting by scraping
c boring tools

Quite a wide range of hand and machine equipment is available. Selection will depend on the tools and the method the turner intends to use.

EQUIPMENT FOR SHARPENING BY GRINDING
Double-ended grinders (Fig 251)

There are many double-ended grinders capable of doing this job. Most have speeds up to 3,000rpm and are equipped with a fine wheel and a coarse one. The wheels should be of minimum 1in (25mm) width and 5in (125mm) or 6in (150mm) in diameter. It is suggested that a wheel with the specification A-54 N5 V30W should be fitted, where A indicates the type of abrasive, 54 in this case is the grain size, N is the grade of wheel, 5 is the structure and V the bond. A written description would read – wheel of Alundum, medium grit, medium grade and medium

251 Double-ended grinder

252 Electra Beckum wet and dry grinder

253 Tormek wet grinder

spacing in a vitrified bond. It is certain that if we are to have a good quality edge and an acceptable bevel, we must avoid a coarse wheel. A good quality wheel will have its specification detailed on the label and a note of the maximum speed at which it should be used. When a machine is new it is a good idea to note the details of the wheel before using it.

Wet and dry grinders

Several of this type are available, and they are usually fitted with a fast moving wheel exactly like those on the double-ended grinder, but they also have a larger, slower moving wheel of natural sandstone which runs in water.

One such machine is made by Electra Beckum in Germany. This has a 150mm (6in) diameter wheel of corundum 60N/150, revolving at 3,000rpm. It can

254 *Tormek motorised grindstone and rubber wheel sharpener*

have, as an alternative, an F16 wheel for sharpening or an F400 for very fine finishing. The slow wheel is of fine grade, running at 120rpm (Fig 252).

Tormek grinders are made in Sweden from natural sandstone quarried in the island of Gotland. The ST-250 has a 250mm (9¼in) × 50mm (2in) wheel and runs at slow speed. The drive is effected by a steel shaft which fits into the chuck of an electric drill; the other end of the shaft bears against a large rubber-rimmed wheel to produce a slow speed ideal for this type of grinder. The ratio between drill and grindstone is 21:1. If the user has a speed reducer, he can choose any speed within the capacity of the drill. The water tray can easily be removed for filling and emptying. The wheel should never be allowed to stand in water since this would soften the stone. The machine is suitable for mount-

ing drill collars of diameters up to 43mm (1⅝in) with chuck lengths up to 80mm (3⅛in). The bore of the drill holder is 43mm (1⅝in) but bushings of 38 and 40mm (1½ and 1⁹⁄₁₆in) are included with each machine. The machine is fitted with a tool holder – which is fine for chisels and plane cutters, but cannot be used for turning tools due to their shape and different angles (Fig 253) but an optional gouge grinding jig can be obtained.

A fully motorised machine has, instead of the drive unit, a rubber-tyred wheel which can be dressed with a cutting compound and used for very fine sharpening (Fig 254).

255 Denford Sharpedge

Horizontal grinders (Fig 255)

There are several machines of similar design to the Denford Sharpedge, but this one has the wheel lying on its side and a constant stream of oil is pumped up to drip on the stone while the machine is running. Available in both bench and floor models, it can also be fitted with a cone at the side for the grinding and sharpening of inside ground gouges.

There are several machines using Japanese waterstones. One, called the Samurai, can be fitted with a 180-grit wheel for fast grinding, a 1,000-grit for sharpening, and an extremely fine grit of 6,000 for the fine honing of instruments. (The grit classification is that used in Japan and does not relate to the Western classification.) A finely finished steel plate, which can be dressed with polishing or sharpening compound, is also available. The machine has a drip feed from a small water tank. The machine casing is in moulded plastic with an integral switch and the wheel runs in a leak-proof housing fitted with a drain-off tube. The wheel revolves at 300rpm and all wheels should be thoroughly soaked in water during use and covered when out of use to keep them damp at all times. They can easily be resurfaced using coarse wet and dry paper wrapped around a strip of hardwood (Fig 256).

MACHINES USING ABRASIVE BELTS

Abrasive belts have been used for decades in the steel finishing industries, yet only in recent times have machines been introduced to use them for the grinding and sharpening of edge tools. I first used a belt machine in the early sixties, made by Picador and called a linisher, a machine much used in larger form for finishing a variety of tools in Sheffield. This machine I still use, fitted with a belt faced with 120-grit aluminium oxide. It runs at 350rpm and its direction of rotation is away from the operator. Very little heat is generated, there are few sparks and the bevels are flat with a very high degree of finish. With the linisher set at the right height for the operator, it is easy to see the action. My tools last a lot longer than those of the man using the fast double-ended grinder, and the quality of bevel could not be improved. The machine has a toolrest but, as I cannot use it for lathe tools, I have it fixed at the far end of the table (Fig 257).

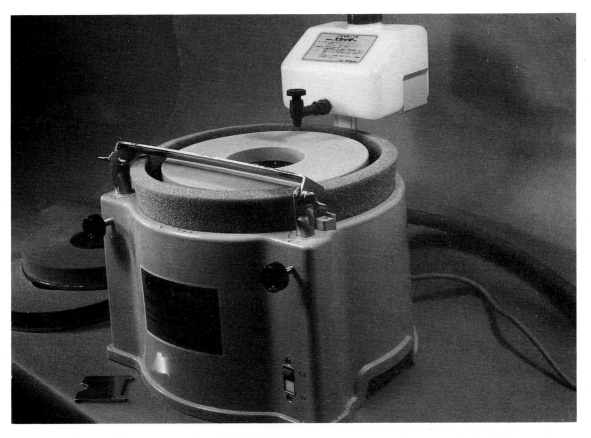

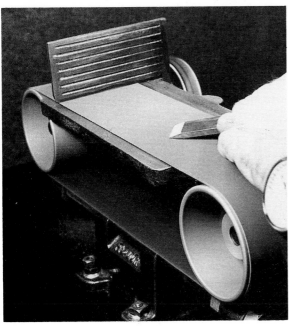

256 Japanese waterstone grinder and sharpener

257 Picador linisher

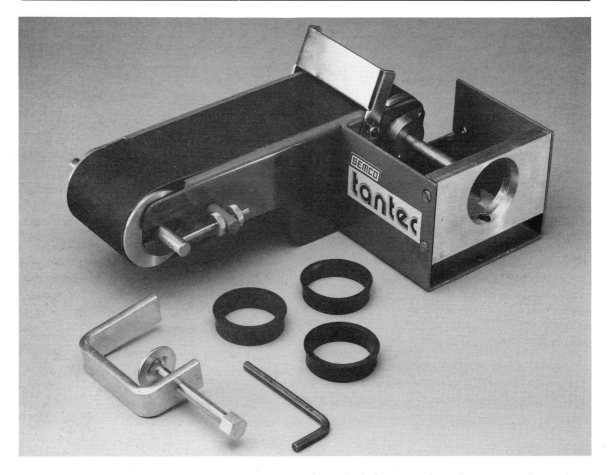

258 Tantec belt grinder

A machine similar to the Picador is the Tantec belt sander driven by an electric drill. Although primarily designed as a belt sander, it can also be used for grinding and sharpening with an appropriate belt. Adaptors are provided to fit most types of drill. A variable speed drill is recommended, but a speed reducer can be used to produce a speed of around 350rpm. This machine also has two fences and it can be used in the vertical or the horizontal positions. It is heavily built in steel and will last a lifetime (Fig 258).

A machine popularised in the United States by Woodcraft Supply is the Mark II sharpening system. This machine uses an aluminium oxide belt 2½in (63mm) wide running between two wheels; the front wheel is driven by a ½hp motor. The idler wheel at the rear is held under spring pressure to keep the belt constantly under tension. The machine can be fitted with one of two tool holders; the tool handle rests in a shoe at the end of a sliding bar which extends to accommodate tools up to 24in (610mm) long. The bar and rest can be fixed to maintain any grinding angle. It is a fully-guarded heavy machine and can be fitted with a muslin buffing wheel which, when dressed with a suitable compound, can be used for final finishing of the tool (Fig 259).

A combined grinding and linishing machine is made by Black & Decker in the Elu professional tool range. This machine has a fully adjustable belt 577 x 40mm (22⅝ x 1⅝in) moving at 1,200m (3,300ft) per minute. The 150 x 25mm (6 x 1⅝in) wheel has a no-load speed of 2,900rpm. A white wheel of 60-grit is fitted for sharpening together with a 600-grit belt. The grinder has well fitting guards and eye shield spark arrestors (Fig 260).

259 Mk II sharpening system

260 Elu sharpening and grinding machine

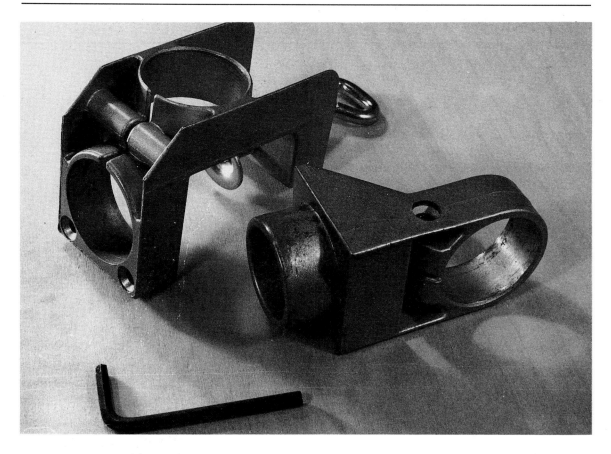

THE POOR MAN'S SHARPENING CORNER

The turner in his home workshop need not buy an extensive range of maintenance equipment but, with a small outlay, his tools can be as perfectly finished as those of the man with a shopful.

A maintenance corner can be set up with the electric drill as the power source as there are several attachments that can be added to any bench to which the drill can be fitted. The Wolfcraft drill holder is typical, and it can hold the drill in either a horizontal or vertical position (Fig 261).

Adaptors, with one plain end to fit into the drill chuck and with the other threaded and fitted with a washer and nut, are readily available. To these can be attached a plywood disc to which aluminium oxide or silicon carbide paper can be glued (Fig 262). Grades from coarse to very fine can be used for both grinding and sharpening.

261 Wolfcraft drill holder and clamp

262 Plywood disc faced with abrasive for grinding
—Vertical
—Horizontal

263 Rubberised abrasive wheel used for sharpening
   –Horizontal
   –Vertical

The rubberised abrasive disc can be mounted in the same way and used either in the horizontal or the vertical position for sharpening (Fig 263).

A stepped disc, the larger step having the coarse abrasive for grinding, and the upper disc rubberised abrasive, makes an ideal sharpening station (Fig 264).

Another idea is to have a three step disc with grades of abrasive from coarse to fine (Fig 265).

264 Stepped disc – one of abrasive, the other of rubber

265 Three-step disc for grinding and sharpening with different grades from fine to coarse

The man with a small motor may care to obtain an adaptor which is bored at one end to slide over the spindle of the motor and be locked on with a small Allen screw. The other end of the adaptor is threaded and, with its washer and nut, can hold a rubberised wheel or a disc (Fig 266).

It is advisable to run the rubberised wheels at fairly low speeds – around 280-350rpm. The drill with a variable speed is ideal since ordinary drills run at between 1,000 and 2,500rpm. Speed controllers can be used in conjunction with the electric drill or can be made – see page 155 for details.

266 Motor adaptor and rubberised abrasive machine

SAFETY EQUIPMENT

Industry has long been safety conscious and, with the massive growth in home electrics and home and craftsman tools, governments everywhere are spending huge sums to draw to the attention of the user the potential dangers. Manufacturers, particularly of electrically powered hand tools, have introduced the 'double insulated' product, which has helped to reduce the danger. Whenever electricity is in use in the workshop great care should always be exercised.

Unfortunately, insufficient emphasis is placed on the dangers inherent in woodworking brought about by the material itself. Wood, like the ladies, can not only be beautiful but sometimes dangerous. With the importation of a wide range of exotic timbers, many of them little known, precautions should be taken against the inhalation of dust, which can not only affect the lungs but also cause problems in the nose and throat. It is suggested that readers take advice if a particular problem is affecting them.

The turner should wear a non-toxic mask (obtainable from pharmacies) – these are cheap and easily fitted and can be thrown away after use.

Probably the ultimate is the Racal series of dust protection helmets which supply clean filtered air to the turner's face. They run on re-chargeable batteries which will give approximately eight hours of use. The filters are long lasting and are easily replaced. All the helmets are equipped with a charger and batteries.

The Airstream AHI includes head protection, Grade 1 eye and face protection, and clip-on ear muffs. The filter and fan are housed in the helmet, and the visor is of the flip-up kind. The complete job weighs 990g (1lb 12oz).

The Jupiter has batteries and charger, Grade 1 eye and face protection, and a weight of 760g (1lb 5oz).

The Dustmaster MII No 2 with batteries and charger can also be used directly coupled to the mains when the batteries are charging. It has Grade 2 eye and face protection with a flip-up visor and weighs just 190g (5oz).

Safety goggles are preferred to face screens by some turners and they can be used over spectacles. The recommended ones have side wings which give added protection. Usually I find after a moment that I cannot see. Yes you can turn wood without looking, but it really is not to be recommended – I suggest the use of an anti-misting spray.

Face screens are better. These are usually made in polycarbonate with adjustable browguards. Some are hinged, and they vary in depth between 8 and 9in (200 and 225mm).

Protective ear muffs are rarely needed by the turner, but where there are other machines in the same shop, he may well be advised to use them. Those fitted with an adjustable headband are best, and they should have foam padded ear cushions.

Woodturners' smocks may not be considered necessary safety equipment, since they only protect your clothing, but a well made smock, which zips up to the neck, encloses ties, shirt collars and the rest. Invariably they have elasticated cuffs which bring the garment tight to the wrist, containing loose ends like shirt sleeves. Obtain a good one which zips all the way down as they are much easier to take off.

ANCILLARY EQUIPMENT

Thanks to those people who have searched the world for supplies, the woodturner now has a wide choice of ancillary equipment designed to complete many articles and greatly enhance their appearance.

EQUIPMENT FOR THE KITCHEN AND DINING ROOM

Pepper mills are mostly made with cast or machined steel mechanisms and in lengths between 4 and 18in (102 and 457mm) (Fig 267).
Salt mills are made in stainless steel or plastic and usually come with tops to match the pepper mills. Lengths are from 5 to 10in (127 to 254mm). Chili mechanisms are similar in design (Fig 268).
Pepper mills with cranked mills and cast iron mechanisms are in sizes up to 7in (178mm).
Glass and plastic bodies make a very useful addition to this group enabling the turner to make a mill with a visible indication of capacity.
Nutmeg grinders are available in two sizes 4½ and 7in (114 and 178mm) and are fully plated (Fig 269).

There is also a miscellany of steel shaker tops, suba seal bungs, optic corks, plastic bungs and cork bungs of various shapes and sizes.

Coffee grinders come in various qualities of materials and design. The mechanisms are similar, but the methods of cranking vary. It is certain that they leave plenty of scope for individual design (Fig 270).
Kitchen and dining table cutlery, generally Sheffield-made in stainless steel, comes in great variety – knives for cheese, butter, grapefruit, bread, steak, carving, with forks for steak.

For the kitchen there are slotted slices, potato mashers, spatulas, cheese cutters, slotted spoons and ladles. There are meat mallets, salad servers, corkscrews, optic corks, and potato peelers (Fig 271).

267 Pepper mill mechanisms

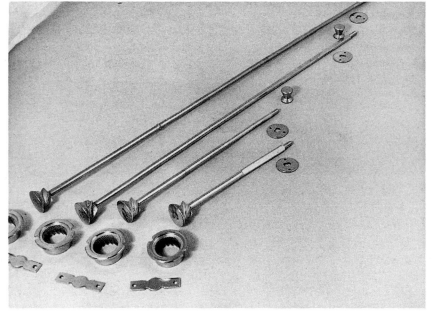

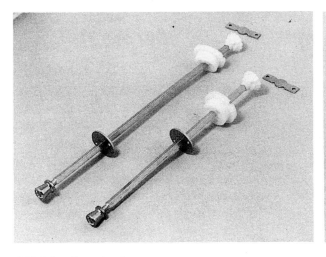

268 Salt mill mechanisms

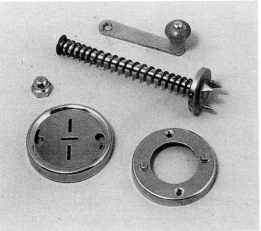

269 Nutmeg grinder mechanisms

270 Coffee grinder

271 Cutlery

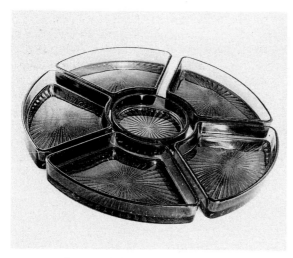

272 Hors d'oeuvre dishes

273 Lazy Susan bearings

Marbleware tiles in 6, 8, 10, 12in diameters (150, 200, 250 and 305mm) are useful for cutting boards, teapot stands, cheese boards, and other items and have become very popular, together with rollers for the pastry board.

Egg and other timers have changed since I was boy – they now come filled with sand of many colours and in timings of 4, 5, 15 min and one hour.

Fondue sets in stainless steel are made up of the pot and lid; pot stand and burner; forks and dots for insertion in the ends of the fork handles.

Hors d'oeuvre sets are available in sets of six dishes, also in one piece together with Lazy Susan bearings in 3, 4, 6 and 12in (75, 100, 150 and 305mm) diameters (Fig 272).

Blue condiment liners in 34, 41 and 54mm (1¼, 1⅝ and 2⅛in) make excellent table ware.

Cheese domes usually made in two sizes, a small one for the cheese set in the centre of a biscuit- and cheeseboard and a larger one for the completely covered board. They are usually available in both plastic and glass.

Miscellaneous items for the home

Circular mirrors with and without polished edges and with bevelled edges in sizes from 2 to 15in diameter (50 to 380mm) are available. The polished ones can of course be inserted into a recess in the front of the frame. Kits are also available for the side hingeing of mirrors.

Pen and trumpets sets are made in steel and plastic, the latter in many colours.

Bud vase inserts are in various lengths and diameters.

Lighter inserts are in chrome and gilt with basic and Piezo mechanisms. The hole for lighter inserts is standard at 1⅝in (40mm) diameter.

Ceramic tiles square and round are available in a very wide selection of scenes, art nouveau, animals and birds.

Lazy Susan bearings (Fig 273)

These have many applications; turntables for the dining table; fondue sets; hors d'eouvre dishes and cake stands. Useful, also, for word-game boards, revolving seats, and television tables. The most popular sizes are – 3, 4, 6 and 12in (75, 100, 150 and 305mm) with a swivel ring of 17¼in (435mm) suitable for a table top.

13

GIANTS OF THE CRAFT AND THEIR TOOLS

ED MOULTHROP

Ed is undoubtedly a giant among woodturners and he has the bowls to prove it (Figs 274, 275, 276). His enormous bowls, some up to 36in (915mm) in diameter, conjure up visions of a tremendous lathe, enormous strength in the man and the tools, which must be different from any others.

The visitor to his workshop must consider himself greatly privileged and must expect to be intimidated, since the blanks are really sections of tree trunks and need a block and tackle to lift them into place. Ed builds his own lathes, drawing on the experience of many years, and they are designed to handle a size and weight unthought of by lathe manufacturers. The lathe is basically a steel shaft mounted in great pillow blocks 3½in (90mm) in diameter and driven by a 2½hp geared motor with an output speed of 80rpm. He operates with speeds between 50 and 120rpm. His toolrest is made from 4 x 3in (100 x 75mm) angle iron, drilled to hold steel pins to act as stops and lever points for the cutting tools.

His tools are certainly different and have been designed to suit his work; even the names are his own – the loop, the lance, and the cut-off tool. They are forged often from salvaged material or from hexagonal tool steel; they vary in length up to 8ft (2,440mm) and in diameter from ⅞ to 1¼in (22 to 32mm). For all outside turning he uses the lance (which replaces the chisel) the scraper, and the gouge. This tool is cleverly shaped and ground to produce a slicing cut when presented at an angle of 45° or greater to the work. The long tool shaft, which houses the cutting piece, gives him complete control with plenty of leverage. He makes his shear cuts using his body a great deal to support and action the tool and can remove shavings up to 1½in (38mm) wide and ½in (12mm) thick.

274 Moulthrop – lance

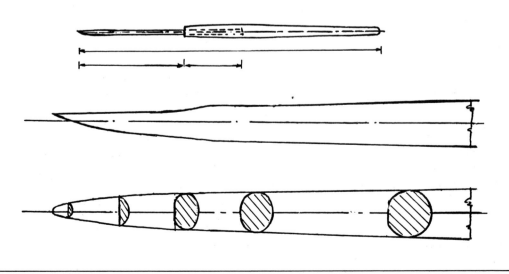

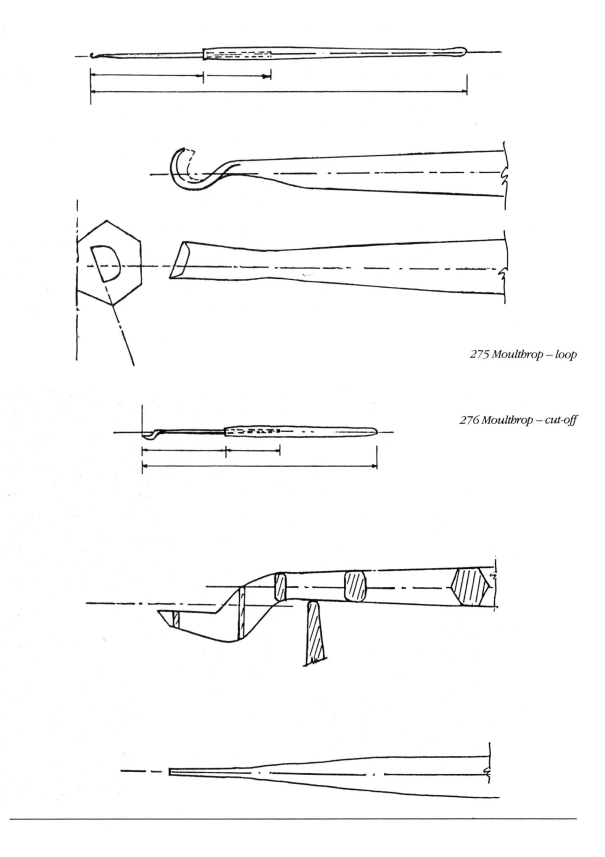

275 Moulthrop – loop

276 Moulthrop – cut-off

To turn the inside he uses a tool, which he calls the loop, that is similar to the hook described elsewhere, much used by the craftsman turner in the last century and still used a great deal in Scandinavia. These hooks have long handles and, after boring a hole in the centre of the work using a brace and twist bit, he works from the centre outwards again levering against the pin on the toolrest.

His cutting tool is long and strong and is angled so that the cutting edge is below the level of the toolrest.

After roughing, he immerses his bowls in PEG for periods of between six and nine months depending on the temperature in his yard, then he dries them for a week in the sun followed by up to three weeks in a drying room. These periods will, of course, vary according to the size of the work. He then moves to a finishing lathe rather like the roughing one but having a smaller motor. Using the same tools he makes finishing cuts as when roughing.

He sands with a flexible shaft and buffs with 0000 steel-wool followed by Tripoli powder and rouge in an oil base.

Ed has his work in many galleries throughout North America. His favourite timbers are tulip magnolia, sweet gum, white pine, black walnut, wild cherry, orangewood and persimmon.

JIM THOMPSON

Anyone passing along Miller Road in Greenville, South Carolina should make a call on Jim Thompson. Jim is a real innovator since he not only designs and makes his own lathes but also the tools (Figs 277, 278). He works on the grand scale in many variations of size and at infinite variation of speed.

277 Jim Thompson lathe showing variator, motor and cakepan flywheel

278 Jim at his lathe

His lathe is large and weighs 1,500lb (680kg) empty, but it can be filled with sand to double the weight. He uses a 5hp motor to turn a hydrostatic speed variator which provides a selection of speeds up to 1,800 rpm clockwise or anticlockwise without any loss of power. It swings 30in (760mm), and some of his vessels are up to 24in (610mm) deep. The headstock bearings are double roller bearings which may be adjusted for clearance by a nut in front of the bearings. Thus each pillow block can be pre-loaded; normal lathe bearings have a set running clearance. In this way Jim can tighten up to take on many of his large jobs which would create enormous chatter on a standard lathe.

The headstock is fitted with a cakepan flywheel on the outboard end, 12in (305mm) diameter. The wheel can be weighted to reduce the vibration, and Jim says that this is far better than adding weight to the lathe itself. With the lathe running at the required speed, he marks the flywheel where the weight must be added. The weights are 10oz (285g) magnets. As the turning proceeds and the weight of the piece is reduced, the weighting may need adjustment. His rests are of solid round bar, and the tailstock can be dropped to the side to clear the tailstock end of the bed where he often sits to do his turning. His lathe bed-ways are of very accurately ground hardened steel, and both toolrest assembly and tailstock run on ball bearings. The tailstock taper and adjusting screw can easily be removed and a boring bar 1½in (38mm) inserted. The bar is slotted at the business end to receive a flatbit. This boring is done between 60 to 100rpm. The tailstock runs on a lead screw down the centre of the lathe bed and is not only used to crank-up the boring bar but also serves to lock the toolrest.

His lathe tools are made of replaceable bits which locate in a slot in the end of a solid steel rod. This slides in and out of a tubular handle to give an extension of length and increase the leverage. The bits are small – $\frac{3}{16}$ or $\frac{1}{4}$in (5 or 6mm); he has in fact taken the centre of the gouge, which does the work, and used it to do the cutting, without problems of looking to see what the remainder of the tool is doing. Using these tools, Jim says that he can complete a vessel 20in in diameter by 24in deep (510 x 610mm) in three hours. He uses them to give a shear or a scraping cut, and they are simple to sharpen and cheap to replace.

His tools are referred to on page 114 and are readily available. He has certainly taken out the hard work and reduced the physical problems created by heavy turning, making it a creative and pleasurable task.

279 Willie Levine's oval chuck – oval vase on the chuck also large oval vase

WILLIE LEVINE

Another giant is Willie Levine who hails from Cape Town in the Republic of South Africa. He has been turning for many years; his works have been exhibited in many countries and they vary from the small to the giant, and many of his giants are oval not round. Willie is a life member of the Society of Ornamental Turners in London. Visitors who have been privileged to meet and talk with him quickly realise that he will not be beaten – problems are there to be solved, and he goes to tremendous trouble in the solving. His lathes have been adapted to meet the need, and his tools have been fashioned to simplify the task.

He long ago mastered the craft of turning cylindrical vessels up to 24in high (610mm), but he had studied Holtzapfel and was intrigued by the orna-

mental turner and the oval chuck. He uses a very large Wadkin lathe made for the pattern maker, and he has designed an oval chuck to fit it. In order to solve the problems associated with this type of turning he first experimented with oval bowls.

The oval chuck (Fig 279) is different from the normal as it must convert one revolution of the lathe mandrel into an elliptical path which the workpiece will follow in order to produce an oval shape. His chuck changed almost from week to week until he had not only reduced it in weight but perfected its action. The oval movement places great strain upon the machine and the chuck and sets up strong vibrations. With large work having tremendous overhang the situation is aggravated, and a different method of supporting the tools on the rest had to be devised. Willie had the courage, the manual dexterity, and the strength to carry out the actual cutting, but to cut deeply and safely he devised a toolrest which some people now call a 'gated' rest; it comprises a rest bar with a further bar above the tool to prevent its being lifted too high or tilted sideways when turning the inside of the vessel (Fig 280). A device similar to this one is the Arnall gated toolrest described on page 98.

Secure mounting of the workpiece is essential for the success of this work; this Willie does by attaching a rectangle of wastewood to the faceplate to enclose the sectional limits of the vase and give a small margin of safety. Careful marking out is needed before attaching the work to ensure that the major axis of

the oval is across the slide direction of the chuck when the assembly is mounted. In this way he can make trial marks and transfer them to the workpiece to enable him to remove much of the unwanted timber on the saw and planer before final mounting using screws and bolts.

The faceplate set up is then mounted to his smaller lathe, and a spigot hole 1½in (38mm) in diameter drilled through the wastepiece. The workpiece is then mounted between centres, and a spigot turned to 1½in (38mm) diameter to give a tight fit in the hole. A clean cut square shoulder ensures a close fit to the driving faces. When mounting the workpiece the marked outlines of the block and the faceplate are lined up as accurately as possible. A dry run on the major lathe serves to check for running accuracy and parallelism at a speed of 90rpm. Final assembly is done using a strong glue and the tailstock for pressure. The glue is allowed to mature for 24 hours.

The turning starts by boring a hole with saw tooth cutters in three steps, the first 6 x 3in diameter (150 x 75mm), the second 4 x 2½in diameter (100 x 63mm), and finally 4 x 2in diameter (100 x 50mm). With the holes bored the assembly is transferred to the oval chuck, tightened securely and fixed with a steel pin through the boss of the mandrel. The hole is then opened up to oval shape in three stages with a boring bar – similar to the smaller ones used by the metal turner, and mounted in the slide-rest. The outside cutting is carried out using heavy scraping tools.

280 Levine toolrest

281 Wood steady with adjusting rollers – hook tool in use

282 The tools of Willie Levine

When both the outside and inside shapes have been arrived at, the speed is increased to 190rpm to enable the finishing cuts to be made. The cutting of the inside is made with an offset nose tool having a round shape and supported in the special toolrest – the extension arm being placed inside the vase for added support. Willie learned the art of taking fine cuts to eliminate any chance of chatter (Figs 281, 282).

To complete the work, extensive sanding is necessary, and for this work Willie fashions sanding blocks placed at the end of wooden bars and shaped to suit the curves of the vase wall. These are supported using the gate-type toolrest. To remove bad scratches the lathe is brought to rest and the work hand-scraped and sanded. He has also used a sanding pad mounted in a flexible drive running from his drill. When the finishing is complete, he applies a number of coats of synthetic lacquer cutting back with abrasives and steel wool – a simple task with a round vase, but quite a problem with an oval one.

All this work needs infinite skill, the patience of a saint, the strength and nerve of a Hercules; indeed many qualities which few of us have. The results however are superb and will long remain a tribute to this giant of a man.

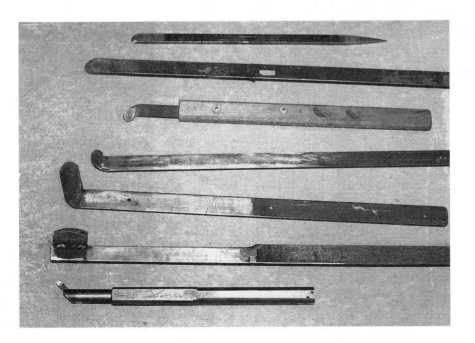

283 Bottle turned in horn by Kurt Johansson

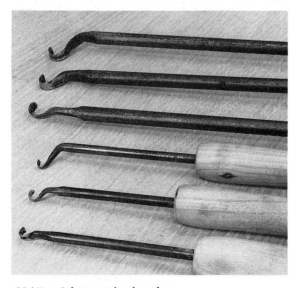

284 Kurt Johansson hook tools

KURT JOHANSSON

Kurt lives in Marieholm in Sweden and is an unusual woodturner inasmuch as he is not only extremely skilled in the craft, but he also designs and makes his own equipment (Fig 283). A master of the hook tool, he has designed his tools in sizes to suit small and large work. Previously I have mentioned that the hooks of some of the tools seem rather large particularly when compared with those in use in the UK in the last century. I have used six of these, and the largest is about ½in (12mm) across – the smallest a bare ¼in, probably 5mm. The larger ones are roughly 12in (305mm) in length; the smaller 6in (150mm). In each size he has one hook which is cranked to give access in narrow aperture work. His handles for the smaller tools are 8in (200mm) long – small by comparison with others. These tools are forged from carbon steel, ground and sharpened on the inside of the hook (Fig 284).

He is a master at turning bottles, and this he does in five distinct stages. All the inside turning is done through the neck. He first mounts the timber in a chuck, turns to round, and bores a hole to the inside depth using an 8mm (⁵⁄₁₆in) drill (Fig 285). The smallest hook is inserted into the hole, and the cavity enlarged to the limit possible with this size tool (Fig 286). The third stage is taken with the slightly larger hook and the workpiece enlarged – again to the limit of its reach (Fig 287). For the next stage it may be necessary to enlarge the neck very slightly in order to insert the cranked tool. He stops the lathe to insert the tool and cuts round the corner, as it were, to enlarge the bottle inside (Fig 288). He needs to listen very carefully and has learned to judge the wall thickness by sound. When satisfied, he completes the outside turning, (Fig 289). The stages are shown with the side of the bottle cut away for clarity. For deeper work he uses the larger tools.

When turning eggcups and small vessels of this kind he uses the smallest hook and completes each turning without the use of any other tool or glasspaper. For bowl work he goes to the larger tools but uses the one with the smallest hook.

Kurt is a clever man who knows the problems of the turner. He is at present carrying out tests on an eccentric chuck and also an oval chuck which he has designed. Kurt makes all these tools for sale, and enquiries should be addressed direct to him.

285 Turning a bottle – hole bored at the centre

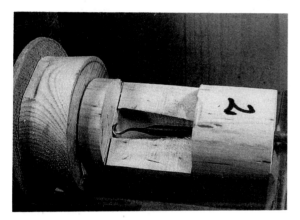

286 Opening out with the straight hook

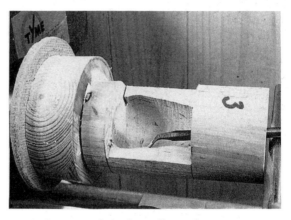

287 Enlarging with the short offset tool

288 Long offset for final inside shaping

289 Outside turned and inside cleaned up

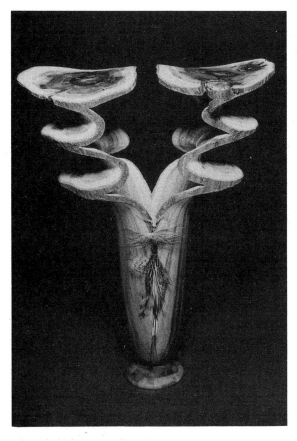

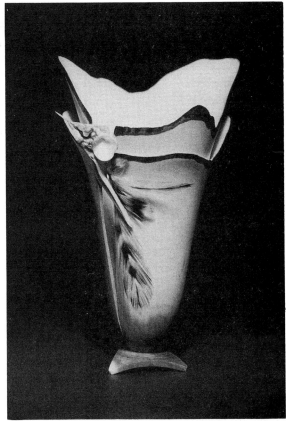

290 The work of Dennis Stewart   *291 The work of Dennis Stewart*

DENNIS STEWART

Possibly Dennis would object to being called a giant innovator, but he is just that. His tools are detailed on page 118 and a close examination of these encourages the reader to see the man and his work (Figs 290, 291). I have little doubt that his work will become legendary, and will be regarded as an exploratory art form since few have ever attempted the turning that he considers 'everyday'.

He turns using his 'designed for purpose' tools and will often stop to carry out a modification to a tool or design a new one. His vessel walls are often translucent.

The turners of the last century, who used the hook to produce three or four bowls from one block, would perhaps wonder at his plunge cutting technique to carry out the same task. Certainly many

will want to question his modified parting tool to carry out this task, but few will dare to question his slicer until they see him at work or try the tool for themselves. He also uses this tool to cut tapered rings which can be stack-laminated for bowls and other work.

Dennis has few equals since he will not be intimidated by the past, the material, or the problems it creates while wrestling with the fantastic forms he unveils. One of his most recent works took three months to make, and I dread to think how much it must be worth. It comprises a fantasy grouping of cylinders of glass, topped with turned wooden domes. Three miniature bronze figures inside the cylinders are adorned with fins, feathers and furs representing sea, sky and earth. He uses many timbers both wet and dry, and some of his work in pink ivory, prima vera and ebony is exquisite.

APPENDICES

A: EDUCATIONAL AIDS – GUILDS, SOCIETIES AND COURSES

WOODTURNING GUILDS

Woodturners Association of Great Britain
5 Kent Gardens, Eastcote, Ruislip, Middlesex HA4 8RX

Society of Ornamental Turners
17 Chichester Drive East, Saltdean, East Sussex BN2 8LD

British Woodturners Association
South Newton, Salisbury, Wiltshire SP2 0Q1

American Association of Woodturners
PO Box 982, San Marcos, Texas 78667, USA

Canadian Association of Woodturners
10 Wyndford Avenue, Nepean, Ontario K2G 3Z3, Canada

National Association of Woodturners
88 William Street, Petombe, New Zealand

Woodturners Guild of New South Wales,
21 Woodburn Avenue, Panania, New South Wales, Australia

Woodturners Society of Western Australia
23 Falkner Avenue, Belmont, Western Australia

Woodturners Society of Queensland
64 Mornington Street, Alderley, Queensland 4851, Australia

Irish Woodturners Guild
Hawthorns, Ticknock, Sandyford, Dublin, Eire.

SYMPOSIA

Symposia are organised on a regular basis by the following:

Craft Supplies
The Mill, Millersdale, nr Buxton, Derbyshire SK17 8SN

Woodturners Association of Great Britain
5 Kent Gardens, Eastcote, Ruislip, Middlesex HA4 8RX

American Association of Woodturners
PO Box 982, San Marcos, Texas 78667, USA

Woodworking Association of North America
PO Box 706, Plymouth, New Hampshire 03264, USA

Symposia are within each Woodworking World Show

WOODWORKING SOCIETIES

The Guild of Woodworkers
9 Hall Road, Maylands Wood Estate, Hemel Hempstead, Herts HP2 7BH

Guild of Master Craftsmen
166 High Street, Lewes, Sussex BN7 1YE

Institute of Carpenters
24 Ormond Road, Richmond, Surrey TW10 3AB

Marquetry Society
67 Pickhurst Park, Bromley, Kent BR2 0TN

Master Craftsmen's Association
11 St George's Street, Hanover Square, London WIR 9DF

The Woodturning Center
PO Box 25706, Philadelphia, Pennsylvania 19144, USA

SCHOOLS AND COLLEGES

The following colleges have various courses in wood crafts – long and short term – residential, and non-residential:

Edward James Foundation
West Dean, Chichester, West Sussex, PO18 0QZ

Rycotewood
Thame, Oxford OX9 2AF

The Parnham Trust
Parnham House, Beaminster, Dorset DT8 3NA

The following run short courses, some with residential facilities:

Craft Supplies Ltd
The Mill, Millersdale, nr Buxton, Derbyshire SK17 8SN

John Boddy's Craft Courses
Riverside Sawmills, Boroughbridge, North Yorkshire YO5 9LJ

John Sainsbury's Woodcraft Studio
Number One, Lichfield Drive, Brixham, Devon TQ5 8DL

School of the Ozarks
Point Lookout, Missouri 65726, USA

Conover Workshops
18125 Madison Road, Parkman, Ohio 44080, USA

Anderson Ranch Center
5236 Owl Creek Road, PO Box 5598, Snowmass, Colorado 81615, USA

Arrowmount School of Arts and Crafts
PO Box 567, Gatlinburg, Tennessee 37738, USA

Appalachian Center for Crafts
Smithville, Tennessee, USA

The International School of Woodturners
647 South Alaska Street, Seattle, Washington 98108, USA

Craft Supplies (USA)
1287E 1120S, Provo, Utah 84601, USA

Russ Zimmerman
The House of Woodturning, RFD 3, Box 242, Putney, Vermont, 05346, USA

COURSES

Information about courses can be obtained from:
The Association of British Craftsmen
57 Coombe Bridge Avenue, Stoke Bishop, Bristol BS9 2LT

English Tourist Board
4 Grosvenor Gardens, London SW1W 0DU, in a booklet *Activity and Hobby Holidays in England.*

TOOLS AND TRADES ASSOCIATIONS

Tools and Trades History Society
275 Sandridge Lane, Bromham, Chippenham, Wiltshire SN15 2JW.

TIMBER

International Wood Collectors Society
601 Burwood Court, East Urbana, Illinois, USA

International Wood Collectors (Australia)
25 O'Donnell Street, Rosanna East, Victoria, Australia.

EXHIBITIONS

The Woodworker Show – London, Bristol
Argus Specialist Exhibitions Ltd, Wolsey House, Wolsey Road, Hemel Hempstead, Herts HP2 4SS

The Practical Woodworking Exhibition – London
1 Golden Square, London SE1 9LS

B: MISCELLANEOUS

ABRASIVE CLOTH BELTS

X 140 Aluminium oxide metalworking cloth
widths   20mm and upwards
grades   320 down to 24

PAPER DISCS

Silicon carbide
diameters   150, 180, 200, 230mm (6, $7^{1}/_{16}$, $7^{7}/_{8}$ and 9in)
grades   800A to 60D
Silicon carbide (Lubrisil)
diameters   125, 150mm (5, 6in)
grades   320A to 80C
also available with self-adhesive backs

Aluminium oxide abrasive cloth discs
diameters   100, 125, 150, 180 and 200mm (4, 5, 6, $7^{1}/_{16}$ and $7^{7}/_{8}$in)
grades   320 to 24

This equipment should always be stored in a fairly humid atmosphere. Pack the discs and belts so that the edges cannot become torn or frayed, or the bonding cracked. Never hang them up in the workshop on nails or hooks since this will tend to distort the belts.

When fitting a belt take care to set the correct tension to avoid slipping under load. Avoid overtensioning since this will stretch the material and cause a break-up. If a belt tracks badly, it may be caused by overtensioning.

FINDING THE SURFACE SPEED OF A WHEEL

Where: C is the wheel circumference
$\left(\dfrac{22 \times \text{diameter in feet}}{7}\right)$
R is the rpm
$S = C \times R$

Example: $S = \dfrac{22}{7} \times \dfrac{6}{12} \times \dfrac{3000}{1}$ ft per min
= 4,714 ft per minute

To check the rpm
$RPM = \dfrac{C}{S}$

GRADES OF GRIT

Grit size	aluminium oxide	silicon carbide
800		*
600		*
500		*
400	*	*
360		*
320	*	*
280	*	*
240	*	*
220	*	*
180	*	*
150	*	*
120	*	*
100	*	*
80	*	*
60	*	*
50	*	*
40	*	*
36	*	*
30	*	*
24	*	*
20	*	*
16	*	*

Marking System

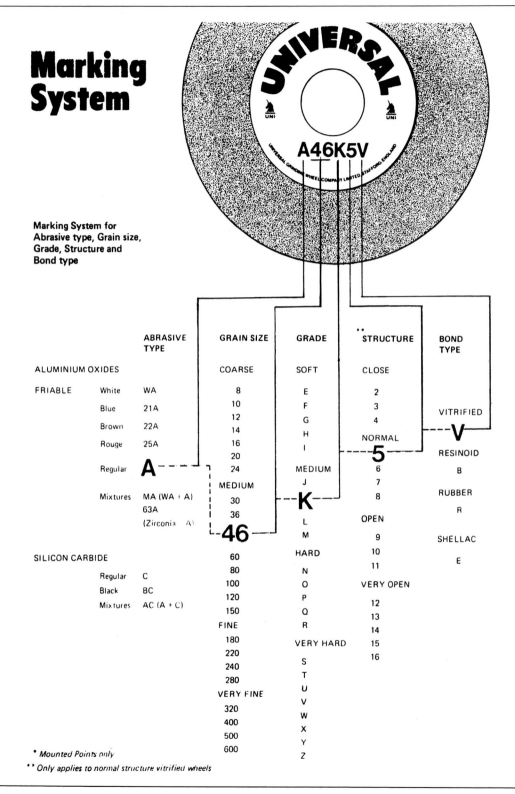

Marking System for Abrasive type, Grain size, Grade, Structure and Bond type

ABRASIVE TYPE			GRAIN SIZE	GRADE	STRUCTURE	BOND TYPE
			COARSE	SOFT	CLOSE	
ALUMINIUM OXIDES						
FRIABLE	White	WA	8	E	2	
	Blue	21A	10	F	3	
			12	G	4	VITRIFIED
	Brown	22A	14	H		**V**
	Rouge	25A	16	I	NORMAL	
			20		**5**	RESINOID
	Regular	**A**	24	MEDIUM	6	B
			MEDIUM	J	7	
	Mixtures	MA (WA + A)	30		8	RUBBER
		63A	36	**K**		R
		(Zirconia A)		L	OPEN	
			46	M	9	SHELLAC
			60	HARD	10	E
SILICON CARBIDE			80	N	11	
	Regular	C	100	O	VERY OPEN	
	Black	BC	120	P	12	
	Mixtures	AC (A + C)	150	Q	13	
			FINE	R	14	
			180	VERY HARD	15	
			220		16	
			240	S		
			280	T		
			VERY FINE	U		
			320	V		
			400	W		
			500	X		
			600	Y		
				Z		

* *Mounted Points only*

** *Only applies to normal structure vitrified wheels*

BIBLIOGRAPHY

BOOKS – MAINLY ON TOOLS AND TECHNIQUES

The Craft of Woodturning, John Sainsbury (Sterling, 1984)
Turning Wood, Richard Raffan (Taunton 1986)
The Craftsman Woodturner, Peter Child (Bell/ Hyman, 1984)
Creative Woodturning, Dale Nish (Stobart, 1975)
The Practice of Woodturning, Mike Darlow (Metaleuca, 1985)
The Manual of Woodturning, Gordon Stokes (Pelham, 1979)
The Practical Woodturner, Frank Pain (Evans, 1958)
The Woodturner's Bible, P. W. Blandford (Tab Books, 1979)
Beginner's Guide to Woodturning, Underwood and Warr (Newnes, 1981)
Woodturning, W. J. Wooldridge (Batsford, 1982)
The Woodturner's Pocket Book, P. Reardon (Fine Wood and Tool Store, 1985)
The Woodturner's Companion, R. Roszkiewicz (Sterling, 1984)
Woodturning, M. O'Donnell (Argus, 1988)
Transvarning enligt skarmetoden, Sundquist & Gustafsson (LTs Forlag, Stockholm, 1986)
Das Drechslerwerk, Spannagel (OM Verlag, Ravensburg, Germany, 1948)
Technologie du Tournage sur Bois, G. Bidou (Eyrolles, Paris, 1987)

BOOKS ON DESIGN AND PROJECTS

Woodturning Projects for Dining, John Sainsbury (Sterling, 1981)
Artistic Woodturning, Dale Nish (Stobart, 1980)
Woodturning in Pictures, B. Boulter (Bell/Hyman, 1984)
Modern Woodturning, G. Stokes (Evans, 1973)
Woodturning and Design, Ray Key

Woodturning, Eldon Rebhorn (McKnight and McKnight, 1970)
Small and Unusual Woodturning Projects, J. A. Jacobson (Sterling, 1987)
Woodturning, Michael O'Donnell (Argus Books, 1988)
Pleasure and Profit from Woodturning, R. Sherwin (GMC Pubs, 1988)
Transvarning enligt skarmetoden, Willie Sundquist & B. Gustafsson (LTs Forlag, Stockholm, 1986)
Das Drechslerwerk, Fritz Spannagel (OM Verlag, Ravensburg, Germany, 1948)
Technologie du Tournage sur Bois, G. Bidou (Eyrolles, Paris, 1987)

BOOKS ON MINIATURE TURNING

Turning Miniatures in Wood, John Sainsbury (GMC Pubs Ltd, 1986)
The Art of Freehand Turning in Wood, W. R. Borré (BJ Miniatures, Windsor, Canada, 1982)
Turning a Bobbin, David Francis (D. Francis, 1985)

WOODWORKING BOOKS WITH WOODTURNING CONTENT

Woodworking Projects with Power Tools, John Sainsbury (Sterling 1983)
John Sainsbury's Router Workshop (David & Charles, 1988)

TURNING BOOKS WITH PROFIT AND LEISURE IN MIND

Pleasure and Profit from Woodturning, R. Sherwin (GMC Pubs Ltd, 1988)

BOOKS ON TOOL MAINTENANCE HAVING TURNING TOOL CONTENT

Sharpening and Care of Woodworking Tools John Sainsbury (GMC Pubs Ltd, 1984)

BIOGRAPHICAL

Master Woodturners Dale Nish (Artisan Press, 1985)

PERIODICALS

The Woodturner, Craft Supplies, Buxton, Derbyshire
Faceplate, New Zealand Association of Woodturners
American Woodturner: Journal of the American Association of Woodturners USA, (Quarterly)
Newsletter: Association of Woodturners of Great Britain (Quarterly)

MAGAZINES HAVING ARTICLES ON WOODTURNING

Practical Woodworking, UK (Monthly)
The Woodworker, UK (Monthly)
Woodworking International, UK (Bi-monthly)

Fine Woodworking, USA (Bi-monthly)
American Woodworker, USA (Quarterly)
Popular Woodworking, USA (Quarterly)
Homes and Gardens – Wood, USA (Bi-monthly)

Touchwood, New Zealand (Quarterly)
Australian Woodworker, (Quarterly)
World of Wood, International Wood Collectors Society Journal (Monthly)
International Woodworking: Journal of the Woodworking Association of North America, (Quarterly)

WOODTURNING VIDEOS

Bowl Turning, Del Stubbs (Taunton Press)
Turning Wood with Richard Raffan (Taunton Press)
Dennis White Teaches Woodturning Series
    Turning between centres
    Bowl turning
    The ins and outs of turning boxes (Knowhow Productions Ltd)
Art of Freehand Turning in Miniature W. R. Borré (Windsor, Canada)
The Thompson Lathe and Turning Tools 1021 Miller Road, Greenfield, South Carolina, USA
The Dennis Stewart Video Stewart-2502 NW 4th, Hillsborough, Oregon, USA

ACKNOWLEDGEMENTS

This book could have not been written without the help of a vast number of people located in many parts of the world. My thanks are due to so many, and I trust there are no omissions. Certainly, but for the encouragement of Nick Davidson of Craft Supplies, the Mill, Millersdale in Derbyshire the book would never have been started. In addition I must thank: Bronte Edwards of Woodfast Machinery at Woodville in South Australia; John Lovatt of Multistar at Colchester; Barry Martin and Dennis Abdy of Henry Taylor Tools, Sheffield; Brian Latimer of Latalex Ltd, the makers of Teknatool at Henderson, Auckland, New Zealand; Joe Snoeyembos of Vega Enterprise at Decatur in Illinois; James Davies of Tanner Engineering at Penrose, Auckland, New Zealand; Frank Scofield of Hegner UK and Schwennengen, Germany; Sven Axner at Vreta Kloster in Norway; Walter Cashdollar of North Western Welding at Lake City in Pennsylvania; Ernie Conover of Parkman, Ohio; Jim Thompson of Greenville in North Carolina; P. and J. Dust Extraction at Chatham in Kent; Gerry Baker of Luna Tools and Machinery at Bletchley; Brian Gardner of Attracta Products Ltd, at the Hyde in London; Peter Hill of Riverlock at High Wycombe; Michael Stanton of Cryder Creek Wood Shoppe in New York; Harry and David Arnall of Berkeley Vale, New South Wales; Rob Ripley of the Hawthorn Institute of Education, Hawthorn, Australia; George Strong of G. W. Strong Enterprises, Dublin; John Farrar of Rawdon Machinery at Shipley in North Yorkshire; Neil McEwen of Multico Machinery Ltd, at Redhill, Surrey; Ashley Iles (Edge Tools) Ltd, Spilsby in Lincolnshire; Ian Styles of Axminster Power Tools, Axminster, Devon; the late Dr E. H. Thomas of Arundel Lathes at Newark, Notts; Paul Chernaud of Scott and Sargeant at Horsham in Sussex; Bruce Pollard of A. Pollard & Sons, Milton Keynes; Boral Cyclone of Victoria, Australia; Dominion Machinery, at Halifax; Denford Machinery at Birds Royd, Brighouse, Yorkshire; Myford at Beeston, Nottinghamshire; Coronet Lathe and Tool Co, Parkway Works, Sheffield; John Costello of Black & Decker (Elu Machinery) at Maidenhead in Berkshire; Anker Rasmussen of Anker Manufacturing at Beaverton in Oregon; Stefan Lundgren at Vetlanda in Sweden; Record Electra Beckum of Sheffield; Hans Lie at Bleikerasen, Asker, Norway and Paul Whelan of Symtec (UK) at Stanstead Abbotts near Ware in Hertfordshire.

Many craftsmen helped – Gerry Glaser at Playa Del Rey in California; Rob Rubel of the American Association of Woodturners; Willie Levine at Cape Town, South Africa; Richard Raffan of Australia; Dale Nish at the University of Provo in Utah; Ed Moulthrop at Atlanta, Georgia; Fairong Amoamo of the New Zealand National Association of Woodturners; W. R. (Bill) Borré at Windsor in Ontario, Canada; Bonnie Klein of Renton, Washington, USA, who designed the miniature lathe (and made one available); Kurt Johansson who made some tools and sent them to me with work at various stages and the tools to be used at each stage; Raymond Geerinckz at Ophain Bois Seigneur Isaac, Belgium; Dennis Stewart who went to great lengths to send me some of his tools and to send a video tape by Vic Woods at Burwood in Victoria, Australia.

My thanks also: to Vivienne Wells, my Editor, and the Staff at David & Charles for their patience, to Sheila Kew for her care in reading the proofs; Ann at Latent Image for such care in processing my film; to my granddaughter Claire for her work on the computer, and to my wife Betty for putting up with me and it.

INDEX

Page numbers in *italic* indicate illustrations